THEY ALSO SERVED

The story of the Sussex Lifeboats at War
1939 - 1945

Martin F. Mace

HISTORIC MILITARY PRESS

THEY ALSO SERVED
The Story of the Sussex Lifeboats at War 1939-1945

© Copyright Martin F. Mace, 2001.

ISBN 1-901313-03-4

ACKNOWLEDGEMENTS

During the course of the research for this book many people happily provided assistance, often without even having been asked. Everyone who helped deserves to be thanked. In particular I need to pass on my gratitude to the staff of the Royal National Lifeboat Institution, and in particular Mrs. Shelley Woodroffe. Without the never-ending assistance and guidance of these people this book would never have been completed. Also to be thanked at the RNLI are Derek King, Sue Denney and Barry Cox, who kindly took the time to read through the transcript.

I must also thank the following people: Mr. Andy Saunders for his help in all matters aviation and Battle of Britain; Mr. Andrew Backway, Station Administrator - Hastings Lifeboat Station; Dr. Peter Marsden - Shipwreck Heritage Centre; Mrs. Mary Taylor; Mr. David Dunstall - Shoreham Airport Collection; Mr. Peter Lindsey - Group Editor, Beckett Newspapers and Mr. Derek Payne.

The majority of the pictures within this book have been sourced from the archives of the RNLI. However, where this is not the case the source of the pictures is shown. In relation to the latter every effort has been made to clear the copyright. Occasionally the source of an illustration used may be obscure. The publication of any picture for which clearance has not been given is unintentional. It is hoped that their use in this book will be seen as a lasting and fitting tribute to the work of the RNLI.

Printed in the United Kingdom by
DC Data Systems, 95 Poulters Lane, Worthing, West Sussex BN14 7SY
Telephone: 01903 525695 email: dcdata@aol.com

HISTORIC MILITARY PRESS
Green Arbor, Rectory Road, Storrington, West Sussex, RH20 4EF. Telephone/Fax: 01903 741941

www.historicmilitarypress.com.

THEY ALSO SERVED

CONTENTS

This book is dedicated to those
past, present and future
who routinely put to sea and risk
their lives to help others,
and in particular to
Benjamin J. Clark,
whose sacrifice was the ultimate.

INTRODUCTION

The duties of a lifeboat and its crew were difficult and perilous even during peacetime, but the addition of a world at war, and the fact that the opposing enemy could be just 22 miles away, only served to make the situation that much worse. Even in the First World War, between the 4th August 1914 and the signing of peace on 11th November 1918, R.N.L.I. lifeboats were launched 1808 times. Some 5,322 lives were saved and 186 boats were rescued from destruction around the coastlines of Britain and Ireland. However, between the 3rd of September 1939 and the 8th May 1945, the red, white and blue boats of the Royal National Lifeboat Institution went to sea far more - in fact some 3,760 times, assisting aircraft and shipping alike.

As described in the War Illustrated magazine of January 1946, *"this was an excellent record for a Service that has never really known any peace; for when the human enemy has been conquered, the chief enemy - the sea - remains defiant and aggressive"*. In fact, the sterling service of the R.N.L.I. during the war years saw 6,376 lives being saved. The Service averaged two missions per day, and some 21 lives saved per week.

As ever the lifeboatmen had to contend with the hazards of bad weather and poor light, but for the duration of the war there was also the added danger of a relentless enemy. Nothing prevented the boats doing their work, so much so that the honorary secretary of the Walmer lifeboat station wrote the following in one of his reports:

"The sea is dotted with sunken vessels, unbuoyed and unlit, and on moonless or overcast nights the men are without assistance to safety during their passages, other than their trust in God and their own stout hearts".

The Lifeboat Service did not escape completely unaffected by the outbreak of war. In peacetime the authority to launch a lifeboat had always been in the hands of the honorary secretary of a particular station. With the outbreak of war this changed. Permission now had to be sought from the Naval Officer In Charge (N.O.I.C.) of the district in which a particular station was located. Not only that, but in the early days of the war, the N.O.I.C. had complete control, and it was only he that could authorise a lifeboat putting to sea. Initially, many of the decisions made by the various N.O.I.C.s were based on a lack of understanding of the methods which lifeboats and their crews operated. Fortunately, the Navy soon saw the force of the suggestion that the R.N.L.I., their officers, coxswains and crews were fully experienced in the demands of rescue work. The system was altered to allow the R.N.L.I. the final decision to launch; though the authority of the N.O.I.C. was still required. Such a restraint often served to prevent the R.N.L.I. carrying out its duties to the best of its abilities.

Perhaps one of the best examples of such conditions relates to an incident that occurred at Fleetwood in 1941. An auxiliary schooner from the Faroe Islands had been at anchor in bad weather, when just after dawn her cable parted and the vessel began to drift towards some of the many submerged sandbanks nearby. Accordingly, the lifeboat crew assembled in the boathouse, and awaited the necessary permission from the N.O.I.C. to launch the lifeboat.

However, the N.O.I.C. decided to allow a nearby naval examination vessel to attempt a rescue, whilst the lifeboat crew watched and the weather deteriorated. Despite the best efforts of the examination vessel, the schooner continued to drift closer to the sandbanks. Twice permission had been requested by the lifeboat to launch, and on each occasion it was given, but withdrawn only moments later. No doubt by now the lifeboat crew were using some of the more pungent seafaring expressions to describe those in authority. On the third request, permission was yet again given, though this time the crew were ready and the boat was launched before any countermand could be made for the third time.

By the time the lifeboat had battled through the worsening weather, the schooner had been driven onto a bank, its crew clinging to the upper rigging. The lifeboat coxswain, realising that there was no time for a cautious approach, ran straight into the shallows alongside the wreck. A heavy sea slewed the lifeboat against the schooner damaging her rudder. Somehow the lifeboat managed to stay alongside long enough to allow the rescue of the entire crew. Whilst it is probable that the Naval authorities were guided principally by consideration for the safety of the crew, such a tale serves to highlight the added dangers with which the lifeboats and their crews were forced to work throughout the war years.

By the very nature of their location on the south east coast of England, the crews and boats of the Sussex lifeboat stations were to be placed under similar pressures and risks as the rest of their colleagues nationwide.

Through the following pages can be found just a part of the wartime work carried out by the Sussex lifeboat stations.

OPERATION DYNAMO

In May 1940, following the capitulation of Belgium, the British government began to realise that the military situation in France was hopeless. Churchill was forced to suggest that *"as a precautionary measure, the Admiralty should assemble a large number of vessels in readiness to proceed to ports and inlets on the French coast"*.

The War Cabinet agreed and put Vice-Admiral Sir Bertram Ramsey, the Flag Officer at Dover, in charge of the operation. Ramsey proceeded to take over anything and everything that could float: cross-channel ferries, tugs, drifters, barges, trawlers, coasters, motor-yachts, schuyts (flat-bottomed Dutch boats that had fled to England on the German invasion of their homeland), and of course the lifeboats of the Royal National Lifeboat Institution. In all, Ramsey was eventually able to muster some 1,000 odd boats, and the Admiralty, with some reluctance, even provided 39 destroyers that would otherwise have been used on the Atlantic convoys.

Operation 'Dynamo', as Ramsey called his evacuation plans, formally went into operation at 18.57 hours on the 26th of May 1940. The results were to be spectacular, far exceeding even the expectations of Ramsey and the War Cabinet. By the 30th May 120,000 men, of whom some 6,000 were French, had been lifted from the beaches around Dunkirk and Calais. On the next day, the 31st, this figure rose to some 150,000 men, including 15,000 Frenchmen, all of whom were returned to the relative safety of Britain. In fact, by the time that 'Dynamo' was terminated on the 4th June 1940 113,000 Frenchmen and a total of 338,226 Allied troops were evacuated - mostly by British ships. In effect, the efforts of this amazing armada had resulted in the escape of nine British Divisions, (albeit without their equipment), in what has become known as the 'miracle of Dunkirk'.

Whilst 'Dynamo' had started removing the troops on the 26th May, it was not until the 30th that the Admiralty actually requested that any available boat should gather within the following 24 hours. From ports as far away as Humber and Poole, the boats began to converge on Dover. At 1.15pm on the afternoon of Thursday the 30th May, the Ministry of Shipping contacted the Royal National Lifeboat Institution, and asked that all of its available motor lifeboats within range of Dover be sent there at once. The Institution was given no other details as to why its boats were required so urgently, but many crews guessed the reason. Having received this request, the Chief Inspector of the lifeboats at once contacted all the lifeboat stations between Shoreham Harbour and Gorleston on the Norfolk coast, and instructed that this request be complied with. In fact this order was sent to 15 lifeboat stations, these being the motor lifeboats stationed at Great Yarmouth, Gorleston, Lowestoft, Southwold, 2 boats at Aldeburgh, Walton, Frinton, Clacton-On-Sea, Walmer, Hythe and Dungeness. The Sussex lifeboats called were those at Hastings, Eastbourne, Newhaven and Shoreham Harbour.

The lifeboats put to sea quickly - indeed the two Aldeburgh boats sailed just two and a half-hours after the call from the Ministry of Shipping. Two boats sailed direct from their stations, the Ramsgate and Margate boats, and were the first to reach the beaches around Dunkirk. The other boats meanwhile had made for Dover and Ramsgate and began preparations for the service they had guessed they would be required for. However, upon their arrival at Dover, the R.N.L.I. crews found that the Navy had no intention of letting them take the lifeboats across the Channel themselves. Instead, the regular volunteer crews were removed and Royal Navy personnel installed in their places. Many of the lifeboatmen were naturally upset at such a decision, but these protests left the Navy unmoved, as did the warnings that some of the lifeboats were not suited to working off the beaches.

So those lifeboats that had gone to Dover and Ramsgate sailed for northern France manned by the Royal Navy, (though some of the boats did retain their volunteer R.N.L.I. mechanics on board). These fourteen boats were accompanied by four others: a new boat just completed at Rowhedge in Essex, a boat from Poole that had already been requisitioned by the Royal Navy, and of course the Ramsgate and Margate boats that had sailed direct with their own crews. In all nineteen lifeboats crossed the Channel and entered the maelstrom that was 'Operation Dynamo'. What they did at the beaches, how many troops they brought off or how many lives were lost on these boats will never be fully known.

The Sussex lifeboats all crossed on Saturday the 30th of May, the day that the Admiralty called for all available boats. One of these was the *Cyril & Lilian Bishop*, the Hastings Lifeboat, its official number being 740. The boat participated in 'Operation Dynamo' under the command of Acting Petty Officer W. Adkin. Its service was commendable, so much so that on a visit to the Hastings lifeboat Station today one will find a memorial to this lifeboat hanging on the boathouse wall. Presented to the station

THEY ALSO SERVED

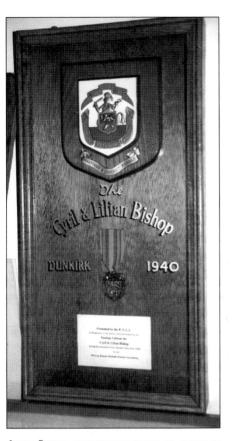

by the Hastings Branch of the Dunkirk Veterans Association the memorial, a framed citation and Dunkirk medal, commemorates the work of the *Cyril & Lilian Bishop* as one of the 'little ships'. (It is interesting to note that this citation has pride of place in the boathouse above an excellent model of the *Cyril & Lilian Bishop*.)

ABOVE: DUNKIRK COMMEMORATIVE PLAQUE ON DISPLAY AT HASTINGS LIFEBOAT STATION

BELOW HASTINGS LIFEBOAT RETURNS FROM DUNKIRK [BY KIND PERMISSION OF THE R.N.L.I.]

Built in 1930 by J. Samuel White & Co. at Cowes, the Newhaven lifeboat crossed at about the same time as the Hastings Lifeboat. With its official number of 730, the *Cecil & Lilian Philpot* was also crewed by a Royal Navy team. This lifeboat stayed off Dunkirk ferrying troops for two days, not returning to Kent until the 2nd of June. Even then it was helped home by the tug *Foremost*, which had to tow the lifeboat the whole distance from the beaches. In his book 'The little ships of Dunkirk', Christian Brann provides us with more detail. He states that the *Cecil & Lilian Philpot* successfully saved 51 soldiers from the beaches, though the mission nearly ended in disaster when she was stranded high and dry by a receding tide for some four hours. Now called *Stenoa*, this lifeboat can still be seen at Walton-On-Thames.

Another of the Sussex lifeboats that can still be seen, this time at Canvey Island, is the Shoreham Harbour lifeboat

Rosa Woodd and Phyllis Lunn. Built in 1932 by Groves and Gutteridge at Cowes, this lifeboat carried the official number 758. Like the other requisitioned lifeboats she was to spend much of her time at Dunkirk ferrying troops from the beaches out to the larger vessels anchored in deeper water off the coast. *The Rosa Woodd & Phyllis Lunn* was also to make three round trips from the beaches back to the south coast, each time loaded with troops. There is also a story that the naval officer commanding her had attempted to protect his crew from shrapnel and machine gun fire by rigging a makeshift wheelhouse from spare steel plating.

More is known about the Eastbourne lifeboat *Jane Holland*, the oldest of the R.N.L.I. fleet at Dunkirk. This boat had been built by J. Samuel White and Co. in 1922 and sent to Selsey. She served here until being posted to Eastbourne in 1929, still with the official number 673. Powered by a single 45hp Tyler engine, the *Jane Holland* was taken across the Channel by a naval crew on the 30th May, and immediately set about ferrying the troops. Things did not go well for she was soon in trouble, as described by the R.N.V.R. Sub-Lieutenant then in charge of her. A French motor torpedo boat had hit her forward in the confused m l e inshore, and whilst the crew set about repairing the damage, she was struck again. This time it was aft, and by a Royal Naval motor torpedo boat! Despite this the crew struggled on, managing to reach about half a mile offshore. At this point the *Jane Holland*'s engine failed and she came under heavy fire from

SHELLED, RAMMED AND MACHINE-GUNNED EASTBOURNE LIFEBOAT THE JANE HOLLAND IS RETURNED HOME FOR REPAIRS. [BY KIND PERMISSION OF THE R.N.L.I.]

German shore artillery and passing Luftwaffe fighters. Having finally given up, her crew 'abandoned ship' and were picked up by a passing boat. A French destroyer, considering her now to be a hazard to shipping, attempted to sink her with gunfire though thankfully was not successful.

As a result the *Jane Holland* was reported as lost, one of four of the lifeboats that, at first, were thought to have been sunk. However some days later she was found by a Royal Navy vessel drifting abandoned in the English Channel. Despite the fact that her bows had been riddled by more than 500 machine-gun bullets, the fore-end box was badly stove in and that she was heavily waterlogged, the *Jane Holland* was taken in tow. She was brought in to Dover, where news had also come of the safe return of more of the missing boats. In fact there was only one never to return - the Hythe lifeboat. Of this boat there was no news for three weeks following the end of 'Operation Dynamo', when it was then learnt that she had been severely damaged off Dunkirk, been abandoned and eventually sunk.

Following her eventual return, the *Jane Holland* was repaired and sent back to serve at Eastbourne, where she remained until 1949. Even then she was to remain in the reserve fleet of the R.N.L.I. before being finally sold in 1953.

THE BARNHILL

A study of the Admiralty map for the coastline near Eastbourne reveals the note 'Debris 3.0 metres' near the low water mark east of the town at Langney. This somewhat undescriptive legend belies the events of March 20th 1940, the date of the first sinking by enemy air attack of a British merchant ship in the English Channel.

The vessel concerned was the 5,439 ton steamer *S.S. Barnhill*, on route to London from Halifax under the command of Captain Michael O'Neil. At the time she was carrying a cargo of copper and other general goods, which included a large quantity of tinned foodstuffs. Built in Canada in 1921 the *Barnhill* had originally been registered to the Montreal, Australia, New Zealand Line as the *Canadian Challenger*. She was then sold to the Ernel's Shipping Co. Ltd. when the name was changed. Finally she entered the service of the Counties Ship Management Co. Ltd whose home port was London.

The evening of Wednesday the 20th March was cloudless, allowing the moon and the stars to shine brightly. A freshening west wind ensured that the sea was lumpy and full as the *Barnhill* made its way eastwards through the channel, entering the final stages of its transatlantic crossing. Everything was peaceful until the *Barnhill* reached a point some six miles south-south-west of Beachy Head - only hours from its homeport. Captain O'Neil himself described what happened next.

"At about half past ten the look-out shouted 'aircraft overhead!'. We naturally assumed that it was a friendly plane, but something about the way in which it circled overhead made me feel uneasy. Then came the first warning of trouble, as the plane started a dive towards us. The Barnhill then shook and began to list, before partly righting herself. A bomb had dropped only a few feet to port! The aircraft then lifted up and dived a second time".

O'Neil was unable to remember the next few minutes, as he had been knocked unconscious in the attack. In fact a string of bombs had been dropped and had straddled the ship. One 550kg bomb hit the stern of the *Barnhill*, penetrating her deck plating and exploding in the number 4 hold, whilst a second unfortunately fell down her funnel. The

EASTBOURNE LIFEBOAT ALONGSIDE THE STRICKEN S.S. BARNHILL [WITH KIND PERMISSION OF BECKETT NEWSPAPERS LTD]

contents of the number 4 hold, a mixture of timber and carbide, caught fire. At the same time the ship's triple-expansion engines ground to a halt. Slowly she began to list to starboard. Four of the crew lay dead and eight more were badly injured (one of whom later died in hospital). Captain O'Neil had been blown from his feet and rolled under some debris and, hidden from sight, was assumed by the surviving crew members to be dead.

The identity of the attacker has to this day never been established. It is believed that a Dornier Do-17 bomber was the culprit. Nicknamed the 'flying pencil', the Do-17 was capable of carrying a 1,000 kg (2,250lb) bomb load and making shallow diving attacks at speeds in excess of 370mph. Even more unclear is the unit to which this Do-17 belonged. Many books state that the aircraft had belonged to the Luftwaffe's now famous 'Kanalkampfgruppen'. However, this unit was not truly established until late June, early July 1940. Goering, the Luftwaffe's supreme commander, had ordered the 'Kanalkampf' (Battle over the Channel), to begin in July 1940, a move which in fact marks the start of the Battle of Britain. He placed in charge one Oberst Johannes Fink, who had previously commanded K.G.2, a bomber unit equipped with Do-17s. Fink combined a number of fighter and bomber squadrons to form the 'Kanalkampfgruppen'. As a result, whilst it is quite possible that the plane involved had been a Do-17 from K.G.2, the sinking of the *Barnhill* was too early in 1940 to be a victim of the 'Kanalkampfgruppen' proper.

The attacking aircraft though had come within one mile of being the victim of RAF night fighters - namely Hurricanes of No. 3 Squadron based at R.A.F. Croydon. Whilst on patrol the Squadron had been tasked to investigate an 'X' plot by the operations room. Squadron Leader Gifford D.F.C. and Flying Officer Ball immediately patrolled the airspace between Beachy Head and Bexhill. Gifford, in Hurricane L1904, saw flashes in the distance, which were found to be the bombing and start of the fires on the *Barnhill*. Gifford later estimated that these flashes had only been one mile distant!

As the *Barnhill* began to list further, at about eleven that evening, news of the attack reached the Eastbourne lifeboat station. The lifeboat crew responded quickly, so much so that at 11.15 the *Jane Holland* was launched and began to fight her way through the heavy swell to the stricken vessel.

When the *Jane Holland* reached the *Barnhill* at 1.40 the next morning she found that a Dutch merchant vessel had already responded to the distress calls. She had picked up eighteen members of the crew, who having survived the bombing, had taken to a raft. The lifeboat took these 18 crew members off the Dutch vessel and then went alongside the *Barnhill*. The steamer was well alight and explosions could be heard within the hull. The bridge had been blown forward and was resting, mangled, on the fore well-deck. Whilst alongside, 10 more men were rescued from the *Barnhill*, joining the 18 already on the *Jane Holland*. Satisfied that everyone had been rescued, the lifeboat turned and made its way towards port, arriving just after 3am.

The sound of the bombing of the *Barnhill* and the subsequent explosions had brought the people of Eastbourne out from their homes - despite the late hour. Once the lifeboat had pulled away with the 28 survivors, watchers on the shore began to report that they could hear the ringing of the ship's bell on the *Barnhill*. It was at 4.45 in the morning that this information filtered down to the lifeboat station, though the report had come from the tug that had been sent to stand by the *Barnhill*. The message read: 'Send life-boat at once for injured man on forecastle. Please send doctor with the lifeboat'!

Captain O'Neil later told of how the ship's bell came to be sounding after it was thought all the survivors had been rescued:

"It was an hour or so after I had been knocked unconscious that I began to come round, to find myself lying on the deck. At first I tried to get up, but could not. My leg was broken, I could not move one of my arms and there was a great big wound in the middle of my chest. The pain was excruciating.

"I was able to piece together why I was there. When the German bomber made its second dive the pilot found the mark with another high explosive bomb. I had been standing on the bridge, which was where this bomb struck. I was hurtled 25 feet through the air before I hit the decking and was knocked unconscious. The debris of the bridge had fallen around me, so I must have taken the appearance of a dead person. So it was that when the lifeboat appeared I was assumed to have died in the explosion and left behind.

"For hours I lay on the deck with the ship burning around me. At about 4am I began to come to. The heat from the fires was intense - like the roaring of twenty thousand blowlamps on full blast! I looked about and could just make out the shape of a tug standing nearby. I tried shouting but no one was able to hear me. Then the idea of the ship's bell entered my mind. The only problem that I had was how to get to it, as I was unable to walk. I still don't know how I did it, but I managed to roll across the deck to get to the length of rope that hangs on the bell. I lifted myself up by resting on my good arm and gripped the rope in my teeth. I tugged and tugged at the rope causing the bell to start sounding. I was then able to hear shouts from the direction of the tug, but it seems that they were unable to get a man on to the Barnhill to help me".

So at 4.45am the *Jane Holland* once again made her way back towards the *Barnhill*, though this time with Police Surgeon Dr D.G. Churcher also on board. It took another hour and fifteen minutes before the lifeboat again pulled alongside the steamer which had drifted north-eastwards and consequently was much nearer the shore. The *Barnhill* was abeam to the wind and sea and was rolling badly. The Newhaven tug *Foremost No.22* was lying as near as possible, but the searing heat from the 70-foot high flames prevented her getting close. Even now explosions were still frequent and the fire had spread fore and aft.

The decision was taken to transfer two of the lifeboat crew onto the *Barnhill* via the tug. The two men who volunteered were Lifeboatmen Thomas Allchorn and Alec Huggett. The danger was very real, and in fact one of the lifeboatmen later commented:

"One moment the ship would be towering above us, showering sparks and molten lead on the water, and the next we would be riding on the wave and be almost level with her deck".

Just as dawn was breaking the tug went alongside the *Barnhill* just forward of the bridge deck. Allchorn and Huggett both jumped, landing on the deck amongst a mass of debris, twisted metal, and the remains of cargo littered around by the explosions. Keeping as much

EASTBOURNE FIRECREWS HAVING BEEN TRANSFERRED ABOARD FOREMOST NO. 22 ATTEMPT TO QUELL THE FLAMES ON THE S. S. BARNHILL. THE EXTENT OF THESE FIRES CAN CLEARLY BE SEEN FROM EASTBOURNE BEACH BELOW [WITH KIND PERMISSION OF BECKETT NEWSPAPERS LTD]

THEY ALSO SERVED

amidships as possible the two men gradually moved forward supported by the master of the tug who had a hose spraying behind them in an attempt to halt the advancing flames. As they reached the remains of the bridge they found the cause of the ringing ship's bell - Captain O'Neil.

Having reached Captain O'Neil, the *Jane Holland* was manovered even closer into the *Barnhill* by Coxswain Michael Hardy, enabling Dr Churcher to shout instructions at Allchorn and Huggett. With his fractured collarbone, double fractured arm, five broken ribs, pierced lung and violent concussion O'Neil was eventually lowered down to the lifeboat. As the surgeon treated him, the lifeboat headed at speed back towards Eastbourne, leaving the *Barnhill*, still burning and unmanned, in its wake.

On reaching land O'Neil was immediately transferred by ambulance to the Princess Alice Hospital in Eastbourne. Here he rejoined the remainder of his crew who had been rescued. He has since described the moment when he was found by Huggett and Allchorn:

"After having rung the ship's bell several times I heard shouts and was able to watch as the lifeboat arrived. It was a miracle of seamanship that the lifeboat was able to get so close to the Barnhill. I then waited as the two lifeboatmen made their way to me. They were taking their lives in their hands doing it, but there is no doubt that I owe my life to those grand fellows. They got me into the lifeboat where I was attended by a doctor".

Later, whilst in hospital the *Barnhill*'s master put his feelings onto paper. He wrote the following passage and sent it to the R.N.L.I.:

"Having reached the stage of nearly convalescent, I wish to state the following as soon as possible, to show my deep gratitude and gratefulness for being rescued from a burning ship, when suffering from severe injuries on the 21st March. Looking back on such matters now, it appeared to me at the time an almost impossibility for anyone to approach the deck of the steamer while the whole midships was ablaze and the deck cargo afire. The two lifeboatmen, whosoever they maybe, certainly showed grit, courage and determination to rescue a British captain from this burning vessel. I would be grateful should these men be decorated and I would be able to look back with pride to that

night, as I was also trying to do my duty to King and Country that fateful night".

Less than three months later on the 11th June 1940, Captain O'Neil was fit enough to attend the annual meeting of the Eastbourne Ladies' Lifeboat Guild. Here he publicly thanked the men who had risked so much to rescue him.

Returning to the morning of the rescue, the work of the *Jane Holland* had not yet finished. Having returned with the injured O'Neil, the lifeboat rested for only 40 minutes before she again put to sea and headed for the *Barnhill*. On board this time were men of the Eastbourne Fire Brigade who on arrival were transferred to the *Foremost No.22*. They then set to work with the tug's crew in attempting to extinguish

THE S.S. BARNHILL FINALLY RUNS AGROUND NEAR LANGLEY POINT WHERE LOCAL RESIDENTS JOIN TOGETHER TO HELP 'LIBERATE' ITS PRECIOUS CARGO. [WITH KIND PERMISSION OF BECKETT NEWSPAPERS LTD]

THEY ALSO SERVED

the fires raging on board the *Barnhill*. It was just after midday when the lifeboat finally stood down at Eastbourne, thirteen exhausting hours after she had originally put out.

Throughout the 21st as crowds watched from the hills around Eastbourne, the *Barnhill* continued to drift north east. She eventually ran aground near Langney Point. It took several days for the firemen to put out the fires, at which point it was realised that the ship was beyond saving. On the Saturday, whilst two firemen were on deck and five below working on the bilge pumps, the *Barnhill* finally broke her back. The precious cargo, particularly that in No. 4 hold, began to spill out into the water.

Even today many local people remember with relish the bounty of tinned food, including meat stew and baked beans, which was washed ashore from the opened hull. The news of these rich pickings spread quickly, with people even wading out into the icy sea eager to gather their share! People were not even dissuaded by the fact that the seawater had washed the labels off many of the tins, leaving local residents with the task of guessing the exact nature of a tin's contents!

In remembrance of the efforts of the crew of the *Jane Holland* the following awards were made by the R.N.L.I. Alec Francis Huggett and Thomas Allchorn were awarded bronze medals for gallantry, with copies of the votes inscribed on vellum. Coxswain Michael Hardy was to receive a framed letter of appreciation, whilst a further letter of appreciation was sent to Alexander Robertson, the honorary secretary of the Eastbourne Lifeboat Station. Each member of the boat s crew was paid a reward of £4 5s. for the three launches - a total of £60 9s. 6d.! The Newhaven and Hastings lifeboats had also been launched, and the crews were paid rewards totalling £16 16s. and £45 19s. 6d. respectively. The owners of the *Barnhill* also sent the crew of the *Jane Holland* a letter of appreciation and a donation to the R.N.L.I. of 100 guineas.

Despite the fact that the *Barnhill* was lost from service, the remaining cargo that had not been 'liberated' was still valuable, and so four weeks later salvage work was started. According to Lloyd s War Loss Books a large tonnage was saved. The list dated the 13th June 1940 reveals that 885 tons of general cargo, 174 tons of cheese, 110 tons of tissue paper, 38 tons of cardboard, and 49 of tin were recovered. As for the valuable copper cargo, some 142 tons were salvaged along with 300 tons of aluminium.

The involvement of the *Jane Holland* with the *Barnhill* was by no means over. On the 7th of December 1940 the Eastbourne Coastguard reported that two men working on the battered wreck of the steamer were getting into difficulties as a result of worsening weather. In a rerun of the events of the 20th March, the *Jane Holland* was put out and made to the *Barnhill*. On arrival two men were rescued and returned to Eastbourne.

TWO OF EASTBOURNE LIFEBOAT CREW, ALEC FRANCIS HUGGETT (LEFT) AND THOMAS ALLCHORN WERE AWARDED THE R.N.L.I.'s BRONZE MEDALS FOR GALLANTRY IN SERVICE TO THE S.S. BARNHILL [BY KIND PERMISSION OF THE R.N.L.I.]

The final call to the *Barnhill* took take place on the 13th August 1941. At about 1.30 in the afternoon the Langney Point coastguard telephoned a report that seven men working on the steamer should be taken off at once. A strong south-west breeze was blowing and the sea was rough. It was feared that the *Barnhill* would soon be awash and the salvage team washed into the water. At 1.50pm the *Jane Holland* was launched, picked up the seven men and returned to her station one hour later at 2.50pm. For this rescue the crew again received a reward - this time a more modest £6 13s.!

Even today the remains of the *Barnhill*, now owned by Metal Recoveries of Newhaven, can be seen at very low tides near Langney Point. Apart from the three boilers (removed recently to allow access to Sovereign Harbour at Eastbourne), there are parts of the engines and metal plating strewn around the seabed. The remains of this steamer are popular with both divers and local wildlife. Such marine life is abundant as the remains of the *Barnhill* provides the only shelter on what is a flat sandy seabed - so much so that crabs, lobsters, plaice, sole, bass and congers are all found in this area.

These battered remains are testimony to the rescue work of the *Jane Holland* and its crew, without whose efforts it would almost certainly have been the case that more than six of the *Barnhill*'s crew would have been lost during and after the bombing

THEY ALSO SERVED

THE MERCHANT FLEET

July 1940 was a bad month for Stephenson Clarke Limited, a shipping company whose home port was London. It was a company with a long association with the County of Sussex, for at the outbreak of the war in 1939 many of its nineteen colliers had been named after villages and towns across the region. Its first loss had been in December 1939, when the *S.S. Horsted* was sunk by a U-boat in the English Channel with the loss of 5 crew members. July 1940 saw three of its vessels suffer in the seas around our coastline. All three of these losses were to occur within just one week. First was the *S.S. Pulborough*, which was sunk during an air raid, followed by the *S.S. Portslade*, again the result of a German aerial attack. The last to be sunk, on the 26th July, was the *S.S. Broadhurst*, sunk in the English Channel off the coast at Brighton.

The story surrounding the loss of the *Broadhurst* is thought to have begun a day earlier on the 25th July when the *Broadhurst* formed part of a convoy heading westwards through the English Channel. This convoy was designated C.W.8, or westbound coal convoy number 8. The convoy consisted of 21 assorted colliers and coasters with two armed trawlers as an escort. It was about midday, when the convoy reached the Dover Straits, that things started to go wrong.

In recent weeks the German Occupation Forces in France had installed radar on the cliff tops of the Pas de Calais. This equipment detected the movement of convoy C.W.8, and as the sea-mist began to clear in the midday sun, a force of sixty Junkers Ju-87 dive-bombers was directed to the convoy. Escorted by German fighters commanded by the legendary Adolf Galland, the dive-bombers unleashed their bomb load on the almost helpless convoy. The trawler escort put up anti-aircraft fire and called urgently for aerial support. Nine Spitfires of No. 54 Squadron from Number 11 Group, based at Rochford, hurried to their aid. Despite this, in the first attacks some five boats were sunk and five others damaged. On arrival the R.A.F. had been able to fight off the remains of this first attack, but the situation was yet to improve.

Late in the afternoon of the 25th, the Germans launched another attack. As the convoy passed Folkestone the Messerschmitt Bf-109s strafed them at sea level and in so doing drew the attention of the anti-aircraft guns on the escorts. At this moment another sixty strong force of Junkers Ju-87 dive-bombers attacked out of the late afternoon sun. Five more ships were sunk and others badly damaged. This was only the start. For having been ravaged from the air, a force of German motor-torpedo boats then set about the convoy. In fact, the damage wrought on convoy C.W.8 forced the Admiralty to conclude that coastal convoys should no longer try and pass through the Dover Straits except under the cover of darkness.

The *Broadhurst* was one of those boats that was eventually sunk by the E-boats. Along with the other survivors of these repeated German attacks through the Channel, the crew of the *Broadhurst* were to be part of a busy day for the Shoreham Lifeboat.

It was at about 7.30am on the morning of the 26th that a message was sent by the resident naval officer to the lifeboat station at Shoreham Harbour. It reported that the *S.S. Lulonga* had been torpedoed - like the *Broadhurst* a probable victim of the E-boats. There was a moderate south-west breeze blowing and a moderate sea as the Shoreham Lifeboat was launched at 8.50am. The *Rosa Woodd and Phyllis Lunn* also carried an armed escort.

Other vessels from C.W.8 that had managed to reach port safely reported the position of the final attacks on the convoy, and as a result the lifeboat made for a position about seven miles west-south-west of Shoreham. Here the lifeboat found a boat that contained thirteen surviving members of the crew of the *Broadhurst*. With difficulty, these men were taken aboard the lifeboat before the search continued. Almost immediately another boat was found, though any sign of the *Lulonga* had yet to be located.

This second boat in fact contained twelve men who were the survivors of the crew of another freighter, the *S.S. London Trader*. Another collier operating out of the River Thames, the *London Trader* had also been a victim of the torpedoes from the German E-boats. The lifeboat crew loaded these men onto the decks of the *Rosa Woodd and Phyllis Lunn*. As a number of the rescued seamen were injured, the decision was made to halt the search and return to Shoreham, the lifeboat reaching harbour at about 10.50am. Thirty minutes later, having unloaded its human cargo, the lifeboat again put to sea determined to find survivors from the *Lulonga*. This second search was to prove fruitless, and it was not until returning to base for the second time that the crew learnt that survivors from the *Lulonga* had, in fact, already been picked up by other boats and

put ashore at Littlehampton.

These attacks were not the first enemy raids at coastal shipping that were to involve the assistance of the R.N.L.I. Earlier on the 2nd March 1940, the Newhaven lifeboat, *Cecil and Lilian Philpott*, had put to sea at the request of the naval authorities. At 5pm information was being received that the *S.S. Domala* had been bombed by the Luftwaffe in the English Channel. Further reports went on to state that a Dutch steamer, the *S.S. Jonge Willem*, was off the coast of Newhaven with a number of survivors from

Survivors of the **S.S. Broadhurst** and **S.S. London Trader** are located and taken aboard **Shoreham Harbour Lifeboat**
[By kind permission of the R.N.L.I.]

THEY ALSO SERVED

the *Domala* on board. At 5.25pm with a smooth sea and an easterly breeze blowing, the *Cecil and Lilian Philpott* put to sea.

When they finally reached the *Jonge Willem*, the lifeboat began the daunting task of transferring the fifty-one survivors from the *Domala*. These survivors consisted of nine Europeans and 42 Indian crewmembers. Many were injured and suffering from shock, so the lifeboat headed immediately back to harbour. With the survivors ashore, the *Cecil and Lilian Philpott* headed back to the *Jonge Willem* for the second time. Here the grim task of taking on board the bodies of three seamen who had been killed during the bombing was completed, before the lifeboat again headed for harbour.

Having arrived back for the second time, the lifeboat crew received a message from the Dutch boat's captain requesting that clothing and blankets, lent to the survivors of the *Domala*, be returned! The lifeboat was, thankfully, still lying afloat and once the appropriate items had been rounded up, she headed back out to sea for the third and final time. She eventually returned to her station at 9.55pm. For their efforts on that day, the crew of the lifeboat was awarded the sum of £18. 7s. 6d!

The Merchant Fleet was not only at risk from aerial bombardment, but were at peril from the large number of sea mines strewn by the Germans throughout the Channel shipping lanes. On the 11th of June 1940 the *SS St. Ronaig* fell victim to one of these devices. This 509-ton British vessel, whose homeport was Glasgow, had been on route from Jersey to Newhaven with a cargo of potatoes and an eight-strong crew. As she began her final approaches to Newhaven, the *St. Ronaig* hit a mine, and began to sink. Two members of her crew were killed in the explosion.

At 12.50pm the coastguard reported to the R.N.L.I. that a vessel was sinking at a position one mile offshore, just east from the beach at Seaford. They also stated that there were men stranded on a raft that was drifting out to sea. In calm weather the lifeboat, *Cecil and Lilian Philpott*, was launched at 1.50pm. On arrival at the scene, the lifeboat was met by a naval vessel that was commanded by Lieut. Commander H.L. Wheeler, RN - who just happened to be the R.N.L.I.'s southern district inspector of lifeboats. He informed the lifeboat crew that one body had already been found. This body, and that of the second crewman killed, were both transferred to the lifeboat to be brought ashore. Meanwhile, the Southern Railway tug *Richmere* had rescued four other crewmen who were all injured. Despite continued searches, no sign of the other two crewmen was found, and so the *Cecil and Lilian Philpott* returned to her station, arriving at 4pm.

This was not the last time that the *St. Ronaig* was to be in the news. In 1959 the Admiralty had ordered the dispersal of the hulk of the 167ft long steamer, fearing that she might pose a hazard to shipping. This order was so enthusiastically carried out with explosives, that the local residents of Seaford began to complain about the damage that these explosions were causing ashore! Her remains can be dived on today, but now stand only one metre high above the seabed.

Sometimes the lifeboats were sent out only to find that the boats were empty. One such case involved the Hastings lifeboat, *Cyril and Lilian Bishop*, on the 13th July 1940. Three days into the Battle of Britain, bad weather on this Saturday had kept the level of German activity to a minimum. Nevertheless two raids were made on Dover, and convoys at sea off Harwich and Portland were bombed.

At 4.08pm, the coastguard reported that there was a boat about one mile south-west of the coastguard station in Hastings. At 4.28pm the lifeboat set out across a slight swell with a moderate south-west wind blowing towards the boat. On arrival it was found to be waterlogged and empty. It was without oars or sails, but there were a few items of clothing and a typewriter on board! Taken in tow by the lifeboat, this craft was taken back to shore. Meanwhile, a further message from the coastguard reported another boat out at sea. This boat, found floating bottom up, was picked up off Hastings Pier and also brought in. The lifeboat then set out a third time to see if any other boats remained afloat and was rewarded with yet another waterlogged and empty boat. Like the first two, this vessel was also towed ashore. Here, it was found that the first and third boats recovered had belonged to the *S.S. Kolga*, of Tallinn, whilst the second had come from the *S.S. Mallard*, of London. All three boats were subsequently handed over to the receiver of wrecks.

Occasionally a lifeboat would be put to sea only to find nothing. Even less frequent, was the gathering of a lifeboat crew, only for the lifeboat to be instructed to remain in port. On the 8th August 1940 this happened to the crew of the Shoreham Lifeboat, the *Rosa Woodd and Phyllis Lunn*. It was reported that emergency flares could be seen out to sea at Shoreham, and so the crew were called to the boathouse. However, it was here they waited, as the instruction to put to sea was never given.

Research shows that it is likely that these flares came from a convoy that had come under attack from German E-boats in the Channel. In particular, one vessel in this convoy, the *S.S. Fife Coast*, was known to have been attacked and sunk fifteen miles west of Beachy Head. A small steamer of 367 tons, the *Fife Coast* had been built in 1933. On the 8th, she had been on route from Plymouth to London with a cargo of sugar. The *Fife Coast* was the third victim of the E-boats, and was sunk with the loss of four Merchant Navy crew and one Royal Navy rating who had been on board as a gunner.

Two further vessels were sunk in the same area as a result of the E-boat activity. The first was the L.M.S. Railway Company collier *S.S. Ouse*. Of 1004-tons she had been carrying a cargo of coal to Cowes. The second ship, the *S.S. Holme Force*, was carrying a cargo of coke, and was on route from the Tyne to Devonport, when she was torpedoed 8 miles from Newhaven. It is possible that the flares reported at Shoreham were a response to these attacks, but that the naval authorities had decided it would be too dangerous to launch the lifeboat in view of the E-boat activity.

The *Rosa Woodd and Phyllis Lunn* was again busy on the 17th May 1941. At 4.36pm the coastguard reported that a German aircraft was attacking shipping about two miles south from the harbour. The vessels under attack must have returned fire, for only a few minutes later a report came in stating that the bomber had crashed into the sea after being seen on fire.

The Shoreham lifeboat was launched at 5.07pm in an effort to locate the crew of this plane or those from any stricken merchant vessels. The weather was good and the sea calm and so the lifeboat made good time to the location of the bombing. On arrival the lifeboat found the *S.S. Ala*, a Norwegian steamer from Oslo - still afloat but damaged. Several lifeboatmen were put on board to assist in the salvaging of the ship's equipment, guns and ammunition. In the meantime, a harbour tug and another steamer had arrived. Whilst the lifeboatmen stayed on board, the *Ala* was put under tow and returned to harbour. Here she was beached, the lifeboat bringing ashore her captain, mate and a naval rating. Others were landed ashore from a naval rescue boat. The lifeboat was finally stood down at 6.30pm.

The Norwegian Merchant Fleet was to keep the Shoreham Lifeboat busy, for on the 11th April 1943, she was again called to help a stricken Norwegian vessel. At 5.45pm

THEY ALSO SERVED

the coastguard service had sent a message saying that a ship was in trouble and sinking some four miles south-east of Littlehampton. So at 6.17pm, the *Rosa Woodd and Phyllis Lunn* was launched.

Guided in by a smoke flare that had been dropped by a circling air sea rescue aircraft, the lifeboat found the wreckage of the stricken steamer. It was the *S.S. Frode* which had hit a mine whilst in convoy. The lifeboat found a man floating in the water, but once lifted aboard it was realised that he was dead. Other motor launches had picked up survivors along with the bodies of other crewmen killed in the explosion. The search for survivors continued until dark, the lifeboat returning home at 10.20pm. For their work, the crew received rewards totalling £13 15s 6d.

On the 4th November 1944 the Newhaven lifeboat, the *Cecil and Lilian Philpott*, went to the assistance of another foreign merchant vessel. This time it was the Polish steamer *Marocz*. At 7am it was heard that the *Marocz* had gone ashore at Rottingdean. It was a foul day; the sea was rough and a strong south-west wind was blowing. Nevertheless, the lifeboat was launched at 7.25am, reaching the scene thirty minutes later. Only then did the rescuers find out that the crew had already been taken off by a trawler and brought ashore by the Newhaven air-sea rescue launch.

Once his crew were ashore the master of the *Marocz*, who had stayed onboard, realised that it might be possible to re-float his vessel. He therefore sent a signal asking that his crew of 22 be returned. Three were found nearby on a tug and were taken back by the lifeboat. The remainder were brought back out by another motor launch which, on arrival, found it could not get alongside the *Marocz*. The crewmen were transferred to the *Cecil and Lilian Philpott*, which in turn transferred them back to the steamer. She then assisted in passing two ropes from the *Marocz* to waiting tugs. By early afternoon they had re-floated the Polish vessel, allowing it to continue on her way.

The *Marcocz* was not the only Polish vessel to require the services of the R.N.L.I. off the Sussex Coast. On the 16th December 1944, it was the turn of the Shoreham Lifeboat to go to the aid of another Polish steamer - this time the *S.S. Chorzow*. With a crew of over twenty, including one woman, she had been on route from Newport to Shoreham with a cargo of coal. At 12.12 in the afternoon the coastguard contacted the R.N.L.I., reporting a vessel in trouble off the coast at Goring. The message stated that the boat was steaming round and round in circles and that her whistle was sounding.

Just over one hour later, at 1.40pm, the *Rosa Woodd and Phyllis Lunn* was launched. The normal coxswain was absent on pilotage duties, so the station secretary, Captain C.T. Keigwin RD R.N.R., went out and assisted the second-coxswain.

After an hour or so battling through vicous south-west winds, the lifeboat reached the *Chorzow*, by now about a mile south from Goring. It appeared that the Polish captain had become unsure of his position, so two lifeboat-men were put on board. They were able to pilot the steamer to a safe anchorage off Shoreham. Before being taken off by the lifeboat, the lifeboat-men added the advice that should the weather deteriorate then the Polish captain would do best to lift anchor and put to sea. Having recovered its two crewmembers, the lifeboat returned at 4.38pm.

This, however, was not the end of the *Chorzow* saga. The coastguard had continued to monitor the Polish vessel, and at 3.46am the next morning they reported that the *Chorzow* was again out of control and drifting. Initially it was thought that the lifeboat would not be needed, but as the steamer continued to drift it came within just 500 yards of the shore. The risk of it running aground was now very real.

Whilst the lifeboat was being launched at 4.57, the *Chorzow* finally ran aground on the beach 100 yards from the coastguard tower at Shoreham. The lifeboat made repeated attempts to get alongside but all were unsuccessful. In the course of these attempts, two of the lifeboat crew were nearly washed overboard by the appalling seas. It was decided to try and rescue the Polish crew from the beach, this eventually being achieved by the use of the coastguard's life-saving equipment. The conditions at sea were so bad that the lifeboat had to remain at sea until 11.20am, before she was finally able to return.

The Merchant Fleet was always grateful for the efforts of the lifeboats - no matter what national flag the vessel was flying. The rescue of the *Chorzow* was no different. Her grateful owners, the Gdynia-America Shipping Lines, sent the R.N.L.I. a donation of £10 10s. in appreciation of the lifeboat's work.

CRASH LANDING

Throughout the Battle of Britain the skies over Sussex were full of aircraft and, it must have seemed to the lifeboatmen, the Channel full of shot-down airmen. With the outbreak of war the R.A.F. had established an air-sea rescue service that was equipped with seaplanes and fast rescue boats. It was these units that were intended to provide the first line of protection for a downed airman in the Channel. In Sussex they established bases for the high speed launches at Newhaven, Shoreham-by-Sea and Littlehampton, whilst air-sea rescue planes were to be found at Shoreham Airport. Later came the addition of the airborne lifeboat that could be parachuted from a rescue plane to a stranded airman.

In spite of the extensive organisation designed to save every possible airman who fell into the Channel, the lifeboats of Sussex were still able to play their part. There is no doubt that the lifeboat crews had frustrating times when often beaten to the casualty by the faster launches of the air-sea rescue service.

It says much for the determination and character of the lifeboat crews in that they continued to put to sea to search for the crews of downed aircraft, whatever the weather and knowing that the mission may well prove fruitless. Nevertheless, of the 1,050 wartime launches by lifeboats to rescue aircraft crews, lifeboats were credited with the rescue of 142 men. As would be expected of the lifeboat service, these men were of every nationality. In the Battle of Britain, men of all the Allied nations - British, Polish, French, Norwegian, Czech amongst them - called upon the services of the R.N.L.I., as well as their German counterparts. As the war progressed, the arrival of the American airforces was set to provide further work for the lifeboat service.

The war had been in progress for just six days when the first aircraft related mission befell a Sussex lifeboat. However, this call, affecting the Hastings lifeboat, was somewhat unique in that it was the actual aircraft itself that was to be rescued!

On the evening of Saturday the 9th September 1939 the sea off Hastings was calm, and the weather clear. At about 9.29pm, the lookouts of the Royal Observer Corps Post at Dungeness watched as a R.A.F. Avro Anson aircraft ditched into the Channel about a mile east of Fairlight. Their report reached the lifeboat station at Dungeness at

CROWDS GATHER AT HASTINGS TO ADMIRE THE BEACHED AVRO ANSON [BY KIND PERMISSION OF ANDY SAUNDERS]

9.35pm. However, the coastguard station at Fairlight had also witnessed this crash and passed their message some six minutes earlier.

At 9.40pm Mr R. Cooke, volunteer in charge of the life-saving corps at Pett also received news of the crashed plane. He called for volunteers to help crew his motor boat, and put out with three men on board. He was in fact the first to reach the aircraft - finding it still afloat with her crew of four sitting on top of the plane. Having taken them on board, Cooke headed back to shore and landed the crew on the beach at Pett Level.

Meanwhile, the Hastings lifeboat, the *Cyril & Lilian Bishop*, had been launched at 9.47pm, two minutes after the Dungeness lifeboat, *Charles Cooper Henderson*, which had already set out. At 10.40 the Hastings lifeboat found the aeroplane, apparently abandoned by its crew but surprisingly still afloat. The crew took the aircraft in tow and began to head back towards shore. On their arrival at 1.30am, the plane was dragged up the beach and finally came to rest high and dry on The Stade at Hastings. Unaware that the R.A.F. crew, let alone the plane, had been saved the Dungeness lifeboat continued to search with her searchlight for another hour and a half. It was only via a passing Royal Navy destroyer that her crew learnt that the airmen had been saved and that she was able to stand down and return to her station.

THEY ALSO SERVED

AN **RAF** SPOTTER PLANE PREPARES FOR TAKE-OFF [© 'THE ARCHIVE', SHOREHAM AIRPORT]

Throughout the following day the Anson attracted large crowds, all eager to catch a glimpse of the beached aircraft.

The busiest period for the Sussex lifeboats in terms of crashed aircraft was without any doubt the Battle of Britain. The first rescue took place on only the second day of the Battle - Thursday July 11th 1940. The day had been overcast in the south, and there was a strong south-west breeze blowing. Late in the afternoon 12 Heinkel He-111s, supported by twelve Messerschmitt Bf-110 twin-engined fighter-bombers, had launched an attack on the dockyards at Portsmouth. They were intercepted near the Isle of Wight by six Hurricanes of No. 145 Squadron RAF, based at Tangmere. In the following dog-fight, the commander of No. 145 Squadron, Squadron-Leader J.R.A. Peel was hit by machine gun fire and his aircraft badly damaged. Peel was forced to ditch his Mark I Hurricane, serial number P3400, in the sea off Selsey Bill.

This battle had taken place under the watchful gaze of the coastguard station at Selsey. At 6.25pm they reported Peel's crash by telephone to the coxswain of the Selsey lifeboat station. With a slight sea running the Selsey lifeboat, *Canadian Pacific* was launched at 6.30pm. At 7pm she found Peel in the sea some three and a half miles off the coast. He had been in the water for three-quarters of an hour and was found by the lifeboat crew to be exhausted but unhurt. Peel himself later described his feelings on his rescue by the lifeboat. In a letter he sent to the coxswain he wrote:

> *"When you arrived I had given up hope. I doubt if I could have lasted more than a few minutes. Your skill in finding me in that rough sea seems a miracle to me. You and your fellows in the lifeboat service are doing a magnificent job".*

A few days later Peel was awarded the Distinguished Flying Cross, whilst the lifeboat crew were rewarded with £11 3s!

The *Canadian Pacific* returned to her station at 7.55pm and put Peel back on dry land. As they were doing this they received news of another crashed aircraft. This time the plane involved was German. In the same 'dogfight' in which Peel had been shot down, his colleagues had damaged one of the Heinkel bombers. This aircraft, with the code G1+LK, belonged to 2 Staffel, KG 55 who were based at Chartres in Northern France. Shot down by Pilot Officer Lord R. Kay-Shuttleworth and Pilot Officer E. Wakeham, both of No. 145 Squadron, the bomber had crashed into the sea off Selsey.

When the lifeboat service was founded, it was laid down that it should rescue all those in peril at sea, whatever their nationality. This was to be the case in both war and peace. This rule of service had been scrupulously observed by the R.N.L.I. for 117 years, and 1940 was to be no different - the rule never being set aside even under the greatest provocation. Indeed the Air Ministry had already expressly asked the R.N.L.I. to make 'every possible effort' to rescue enemy airmen. So it was that as soon as Peel had been put ashore the *Canadian Pacific* turned round and set out to sea again. The time now was 8.10pm.

They headed for the reported position of the crashed bomber, some five miles south of the Owers light-vessel. Reaching here just after 9pm, they immediately set about a systematic search. Finding nothing but a large patch of oil, the lifeboat crew gave up the search and returned to her station at 10.30pm.

Unbeknown to her crew, the German airmen had already been rescued. Four had survived the crash, whilst one, Offz. W. Muller, was killed. One of the survivors, Oberfw. H. Schluter, was so badly injured that he died later the same day. Both Muller and Schluter now lie in the graveyard of St. Andrews church, Tangmere.

Throughout the months of July and August 1940, the height of the Battle of Britain, it was the Selsey and Shoreham lifeboats that were to bear the brunt of the activity in Sussex with a constant stream of calls to ditched aircraft - both Allied and German. Come September, however, the action seemed to have drifted east along the coast.

On the 5th September German attacks were made across the south of England, with ineffectual raids being made against the aircraft factories at Brooklands, Surrey, and on targets in London. At 3.38pm, people on the seafront and the cliff tops at Hastings were rewarded with the spectacle of a German plane being chased out to sea by an R.A.F. Spitfire.

The German fighter, a Messerschmitt Bf-109E-1 single engined fighter, had already been damaged in an earlier combat over the Isle of Sheppey, but had tried to make for the safety of the French Coast. The second attack over Hastings was, however, to prove fatal and the aircraft from 9th Staffel JG53, ditched in the Channel southwest of Hastings. As the German pilot, Fw. A. Ochenskuhn, took to his dinghy, Pilot Officer J. Zurakowski, a Pole serving with No. 234 Squadron, banked his Spitfire and headed back to his airfield at St.Eval.

The Hastings lifeboat, the *Cyril & Lilian Bishop*, was launched immediately and headed off to retrieve Ochenskuhn. They found him, unhurt, twelve miles south of Hastings, and he was returned to shore at 5pm.

The *Cyril & Lilian Bishop* was again in action on the 27th September 1940. This day saw the Luftwaffe suffer some of its worst losses, with the fourth worst casualty figures for the whole of the Battle of Britain. At 5.25pm the coastguard reported that a German aeroplane had come down in the sea, about a quarter of a mile southwest of the bathing pool at St.Leonards. The lifeboat was launched at 5.37pm with the honorary secretary, Commander W. Highfield O.B.E. R.N., going out with her. As she raced her way south through a slight sea, a second report was received stating that a further German plane had crashed in flames six miles further south.

On arrival at the location of the first crash, the lifeboat crew came across one survivor. Gefr. J. Feichtmayer who was badly wounded, and despite having been in the water for two hours, was able to tell the crew of the *Cyril & Lilian Bishop* what had happened. His aircraft, a Junkers Ju-88 bomber from 5th Staffel KG55, with the serial number 4117 and code 3Z+DN, had been badly damaged by RAF fighters whilst trying to bomb London. The victor was Flying Officer W. Urbanowicz of No. 303 Squadron, a Pole flying a Hurricane from RAF Northolt.

Unable to make France, the German plane had crashed in the Channel. Oberlt. F. Ziel and Fw. F. Niederer had managed to escape from the ditched bomber, but both were subsequently found to have drowned. These were the two airmen who Feichtmayer told the lifeboat crew 'had been lost'. The final airman was believed to have been unable to escape from the aircraft before it sank. With the survivor on board, the lifeboat headed back to shore, arriving at 6pm. On the 21st October the body of one of the 'lost' men, the observer Franz Niederer, was washed ashore near Battle, whilst on the 22nd, the body of the pilot, Friederich Ziel, was found on the beach at

[By kind permission of the R.N.L.I.]

Hastings. He now lies in the grounds of Hastings Cemetery, though the date of his death is incorrectly shown as the day on which his body was washed ashore. As for the second burning plane reported to the Hastings lifeboat, no trace was found of her crew, though it is likely that this aircraft was another Ju-88 bomber from KG55.

Three days later on the 30th, it was the turn of the *Canadian Pacific*, the Selsey lifeboat, to be sent to a stricken Junkers Ju-88. Whilst attempting to bomb Portsmouth, Junkers Ju-88 A1, serial number 2063, was shot down by No. 602 Squadron Spitfires. Fatally hit, the bomber was seen to dive through the clouds and crash into the sea some 3 miles south-west of Selsey. The lifeboat was informed of the crash at 4.19pm, and put to sea in only eleven minutes. The water was choppy, and a strong north-east breeze was blowing. As the *Canadian Pacific* closed on the location of the crash, her crew saw a seaplane from the air-sea rescue service already landed on the water. At this point the lifeboat crew came across a body floating in the water, which they took on board. As they did this, the seaplane took off again. The lifeboat returned to Selsey, arriving at 6pm, where the body was handed over to the Police. The dead airman picked up by the lifeboat crew was Gefr. Rudolf Penka. His body, along with that of fellow crewmember Gefr. Max Hoppert (the air-gunner), whose body was washed ashore on October 15th, now lies in St. Nicholas's Churchyard at West Thorney. No trace has ever been found of the two other airmen.

Not all calls to crashed German aircraft were to result in the finding of a plane's crew. Such an occurrence happened on the 2nd September 1942. At 9.58am it was reported that a parachute had been seen to drop some twelve miles southwest of Hastings. The *Cyril & Lilian Bishop* was launched and joined what was rapidly becoming a full-scale air-sea rescue operation. On reaching the approximate location of the parachute, the lifeboat found that a seaplane was already searching. As it did this, the seaplane dropped a smoke-marker to which the lifeboat headed.

Nothing was found here, or at the position supplied by the coastguard, so the lifeboat turned and headed for Hastings. As she motored through a slight sea, the crew found a German parachute, and shortly after a petrol tank from a British aircraft. A motorboat that had been assisting with the search also found nothing.

It was not only the regular Sussex lifeboats that were kept busy by aircraft falling into the waters of the English Channel. On the 3rd February 1944 a reserve lifeboat, the *Hearts of Oak*, was launched from the lifeboat station at Selsey. The crew was already mustered at the lifeboat station when they watched a Hawker Typhoon fighter-bomber flying low across the water. From its speed and height the lifeboatmen knew that the plane was in trouble, and so it was no surprise when, moments later, the Typhoon crashed. Ten minutes later, at 3.50pm, the *Hearts of Oak*, which was on temporary duty at Selsey, was underway.

As the sea was relatively calm, tickled only by a moderate southwest wind, it did not take the lifeboat long to cover the three-quarters of a mile to the crashed plane. On arrival they found the pilot floating in his dinghy and within twenty minutes of crashing he was pulled onto the decks of the lifeboat. The pilot had fared better than his plane, which had by now sunk from sight. He was suffering from the cold and shock, and a cut to his head.

On the 27th July 1941 a pilot was rescued from his dinghy by a shore-boat that had been launched from the beach at Bexhill. It was at high tide at 2.55pm that the coastguard reported that a British plane had come down and that its pilot had taken to his rubber life raft. Two men put to sea in the shore-boat and covered the one and a half

miles to the pilot through good seas. The R.N.L.I. records state that it had been a Spitfire that had come to grief, but R.A.F. records show only one fighter lost on the 27th, a Mark II Hurricane from No. 242 Squadron. Whilst his plane, number Z3563, was lost the records indicate that Flight Sgt. G.A. Prosser was saved following his tangle with German Messerschmitt 109 fighters.

On the 7th December 1941 the Japanese launched an all out attack on the American Fleet at Pearl Harbour. Almost immediately American forces began to muster on the shores of Britain, providing yet more work for the boats of the R.N.L.I. One of the first rescues involving an American aircraft took place on the 6th September 1943, some half a mile from the beach at Bexhill.

At 12.40pm the police and coastguard both reported that an aircraft was down in the sea. The aircraft, a Boeing B-17 Flying Fortress bomber, was about a quarter of a mile from the shore. The *Cyril & Lilian Bishop* was launched from Hastings at 1.17pm under the charge of the second coxswain, followed closely by the Eastbourne lifeboat *Jane Holland*. Arriving at the scene of the crash, the only item found was a quantity of photographic equipment attached to a parachute that was taken onboard the *Cyril & Lilian Bishop*. The lifeboat crews could also see that a rubber dinghy had been washed onto the beach nearby. It was at this point that the lifeboats were informed that they were not the only people involved in this rescue effort!

Having crashed into the water, five of the American crew had managed to clamber into a dinghy, whilst the remaining five clung to the outside of another. Despite the fine weather the rollers were big, with the American airmen having a struggle to remain afloat. One shore-boat was eventually able to reach the first dinghy with the airmen clinging to the edges, and they were plucked from the water. The other airmen had managed to reach the shore under their own steam by making use of the small emergency paddles fitted to the dinghy.

As this had all been unfolding under the gaze of watchers on the shore two other 15-foot rowing boats had also been launched, crewed by soldiers from 301 Battery, Royal Artillery. The first, manned by two soldiers, was almost at once washed ashore by the heavy swell. The second, with three crew, fared only marginally better. No sooner had it got away from the beach then the oars broke, and this boat was also forced back onto the beach!

At the same time, further east in Pevensey Bay, rescuers were fighting their way to two other Fortresses that had also ditched off the coast! With the lifeboats occupied off Bexhill, the 28-foot trawler *Eva* had set out with her crew of four. They rescued six airmen from a dinghy, another who was clinging onto the side, and three who had remained on the wings of one of the bombers. Another fishing boat, the 20-foot *N.N.60*, went to the last Fortress. On board was the Assistant Chief Constable A.G. Cargill. Seven airmen were plucked to safety, whilst another still lay injured on one of the aircraft s wings. The *N.N.60* got as close as her master dared at which point Cargill jumped across onto the plane. Here he placed the injured airmen in a dinghy and jumped back onto the trawler. The dinghy with the injured airmen was then taken in tow.

Only two Americans were now outstanding. Yet another fishing boat arrived on scene, this time with a crew of five - two civilians and three soldiers. As they approached the second plane they came across the last two airmen and lifted them on board. With a total of thirty aircrew saved all the boats returned to shore, leaving the bombers to sink slowly beneath the waves.

Rewards were paid to all the rescuers, who even included a local caf proprietor. One of the soldiers returned his reward to the Institution as a donation.

RAF Spitfire and Walrus aircraft on standby at Shoreham Airport [© 'The Archive' Shoreham Airport]

THEY ALSO SERVE

For the remainder of the War, American aircraft were frequently reported to have crashed in the Channel. Today many provide good dive sites. A good example is the remains of a Fortress that lies on the seabed 200 yards from the end of Hastings Pier. Whether this is one of the aircraft involved in the epic rescue described above is not known. Lying at a depth of 12 metres the wreckage, including two engines resting on the bottom, sports abundant marine life and is often described as a 'wonderful dive for novices'. Fortresses, however, were not the only American bombers to find a watery grave off the Sussex coast.

On the 30th of December 1943 a United States Consolidated B-24 Liberator bomber crashed in Pevensey Bay, one and a half miles south-west of the coastguard station. Almost as soon as the plane had hit the icy-cold water, four Pevensey Bay fishermen launched the fishing boat *Dolphin*. On reaching the wreckage, six airmen were pulled on board. The fishermen were informed that the remaining four crew had been lost in the aeroplane. As the *Dolphin* turned for shore, another motorboat arrived. As this second boat turned to follow the *Dolphin*, one of the airmen's hats fouled their propeller. The result was a long, hard row back to shore! To the crew of the *Dolphin*, the R.N.L.I. paid a reward of £2 10s. whilst the three crew of the second boat received £1 10s. For the fuel used by both boats, a payment of £4 was made.

Today, it is still possible to dive on the remains of a Liberator bomber that can be found lying in ten metres of water in Pevensey Bay. The only problem however, is that the aircraft is upside down. Divers report that the fuselage is generally intact but flattened, and that the wings and engines may still be seen resting on the seabed. From the location of this wreckage, it is almost certain that these are the remains of the aircraft to which the *Dolphin* headed on that December day.

The American Air Forces in Britain were fully aware of the services that the R.N.L.I. provided to its men who fell into the waters around our shores. So much so, that in late 1944 the R.N.L.I. published a note sent to it by an American Squadron Leader:

> "The fine work being accomplished by the men of the Lifeboat Service has on several occasions been brought to my personal attention and the attention of the men under my command. It is with deep gratitude that the enclosed money is sent".

As can already be seen in this chapter, there is no shortage of German aircraft littering the seabed. Further victims fell on the 18th August 1940, a date that has gone down in history as the 'Armageddon' of the Battle of Britain. This was the day that the Luftwaffe tried to smash the R.A.F., with the skies over southern England full of frantic aerial activity.

At 2.30pm the coastguard station at Selsey again looked on as one such air battle was acted out five miles south-west of Selsey Bill. Within a few minutes, at least five aircraft were reported down. With a moderate breeze but a choppy sea, the *Canadian Pacific* was launched at 2.40pm. Directed by the coastguard, the lifeboat crew found two airmen floating in the water. Despite their wounds, both were taken on board the lifeboat. Oberfw. G Riergler and Gefr. O. Langwost were the crew of a Junkers Ju-87 Stuka that had been shot down whilst dive-bombing the airfield at Thorney Island. A continued search revealed nothing else and the lifeboat returned to her station at 5pm, when the two prisoners, slightly worse for wear, were handed over to the military authorities.

Not all launches had the added advantage of daylight. In the early hours of Sunday the 25th August 1940 the Hastings lifeboat was called for and launched at 2am. The coastguard had, twenty-eight minutes earlier, given a report of a crashed aircraft off Hastings. It was 3.20am when the *Cyril & Lilian Bishop* arrived off Ecclestone Glen. Unable to see anything, the crew stopped the engines, allowing the lifeboat to remain silent. Remarkably a cry was heard, and its source was eventually found.

Fw. A. Schmaderer had been one of five crew-members of a Heinkel He-111 bomber, G1+CT, which had been tasked to bomb the R.A.F. base at Harwell. Attempting to return to France the bomber had become trapped in searchlights near the south coast. Guided by these beams of light, Flight Lieut. J.G. Saunders of No. 615 Squadron, flying a Hurricane night-fighter, closed in and engaged his target. Fatally hit, the bomber crashed into the sea 1 mile off Hastings. Before the aircraft had exploded and burnt out, Schmaderer had been able to escape, though he was the only survivor. Picked up by the lifeboat, he was put ashore at 3.45am and handed over to the military authorities.

As the war progressed, the air-sea rescue service, equipped with high speed launches and supported by a variety of aircraft, became more established. The result was that it became more and more common for the Sussex lifeboats to work alongside these units in the rescue of crashed airmen. Part of this military rescue service was No. 277 (Air-Sea Rescue) Squadron, based at Shoreham Airport. Its operational log for 1944 gives examples of the collaboration between the military and the R.N.L.I. in their rescues. No. 277 squadron was one of seven U.K. based air-sea rescue units - the four others being located in the Middle-East. By the end of the war, it was the most successful of the eleven Squadrons, rescuing 598 survivors. Whilst the Supermarine Walrus was the mainstay of many of these units, other types, such as the Supermarine Sea Otter and the Spitfire, were employed.

It was at 9.12am on the 11th June 1944 that the coastguard asked the honorary secretary of the Eastbourne lifeboat station if the *Jane Holland* could be launched to an aircraft that had come down in the sea two miles south-south-east of the lookout station. At that point a Supermarine Walrus amphibious aircraft of No.277 Squadron was also tasked to the rescue operation. At the time it had been on patrol south of the Isle of Wight, but immediately made for the position of the crashed aircraft, given as 6 miles east of Beachy Head. The information also stated that the crashed aircraft was an American Flying Fortress.

On the arrival of the Walrus, it's crew found an R.A.F. high-speed launch picking up the airmen, helped by a Supermarine Sea Otter, which was circling the wreckage. Five of the Americans had survived, whilst two had died. One of the air-sea rescue aircraft was vectored to a position where a dinghy was reported in the water. On arrival Sqn.Ldr. L.J. Brown found two K-type dinghies tied together and a dead airman lying in one.

Meanwhile back on shore, and in an effort to save time, the coxswain of the *Jane Holland* put out with the mechanic and four other men in his own fishing boat. They reached the air-sea rescue units where they took on board an injured airman, transferred from the No.277 Squadron Walrus. Satisfied that nothing else could be done, the fishing boat headed back for shore, arriving at 11.50am. The R.N.L.I. paid rewards to the lifeboat crew that went out of £3 15s; to the helpers £2 0s. 6d.; whilst for the fuel used, a payment of 2s. 6d.

Another rescue, for which the RNLI paid rewards, occurred on the 5th March 1944. Shortly after two in the afternoon, two men in the fishing boat *FE.152* were trawling in

Rye Bay. On hearing a burst of machine-gun fire, their attention was drawn to an American Thunderbolt fighter. As they watched, the pilot baled out and parachuted into the calm sea. Lashing a rubber buoy to the towrope of their trawl, the two men abandoned their catch and headed towards the pilot. It took them fifteen minutes to reach him, and on arrival found him very cold, so much so that he was unable to speak. He was immediately lifted onto the fishing boat, along with his dinghy and oxygen bottle, the two fishermen then turning and heading for shore.

Not knowing that the pilot had been saved, the air-sea rescue services had already been alerted. At Shoreham, an aircraft of No.277 Squadron was scrambled and instructed to make for a point two miles south of Rye Harbour. A high-speed launch was also on its way. First to arrive was the seaplane, only to find that they had been beaten to the spot by the *FE.152*. Soon after the launch intercepted the fishing boat on its way to Rye. They came alongside and the pilot was transferred across. Its good work done, the *FE.152* returned to her trawling gear, only to find that all the fish had been lost! Nevertheless, the R.N.L.I. paid her crew the reward of £10 for the escaped fish, and 2s. 6d. for the fuel that had been used.

The last rescue to be described in this chapter is different in that it illustrates the point that even for the R.N.L.I., not everything went according to the *'best laid plans of mice and men!*

In the early days of the war, on the 20th October 1939, the Bognor Police reported to the coastguard that a naval aircraft had crashed into the Channel just off the beach at Bognor. Thankfully the sea was smooth, and at 1.55am the Selsey lifeboat, *Canadian Pacific*, was launched. Soon after, the lifeboat crew found the aircraft on the water close to the beach at Felpham. At this point, however, things started to go wrong. A problem developed with the engine of the *Canadian Pacific*, ensuring that she was no longer able to reverse. As a result she was unable to reach the plane, before she herself went aground on a sandbank. Seeing the problems that the lifeboat was suffering, the airmen took matters into their own hands, jumping from the plane and swimming ashore! After much effort the lifeboat was eventually able to extricate herself and returned to her station.

A NAVY IN TROUBLE

The outbreak of war sparked a seemingly never-ending increase in military shipping movements in the waters of the south coast. With such an increase in naval traffic came more frequent calls to assist the vessels of the Royal Navy.

One such call came on the 13th June 1940. At 7.45pm a violent explosion was heard throughout the port and town of Newhaven which appeared to have come from out at sea. Gradually it became apparent to the Naval Officer In Charge, (N.O.I.C.), at Newhaven that a naval vessel had been the cause. In fine weather and with a calm sea the minesweeper *H.M.S. Ocean Sunlight* had hit a mine. The resulting explosion caused such horrendous damage that the vessel immediately began taking water, sinking quite rapidly within 800 yards of the harbour arm.

At 7.57pm the Newhaven lifeboat, the *Cecil & Lilian Philpott*, was launched. Arriving at the scene of the explosion, the lifeboat crew found that their services were no longer needed. A naval tug, *H.M.S. Forwood*, had also made for the stricken vessel. Arriving first, she had rescued the five crew-members, from a total of fourteen, that had survived the explosion. At the request of the N.O.I.C., however, the lifeboat crew salvaged some of the equipment from the minesweeper, and returned it to shore.

Years later in 1959 the 131-ton drifter, originally built in 1929, was again the source of explosions that resounded across Newhaven. The wreckage had become a hazard to shipping, resulting in the navy being requested to break it up. So enthusiastically was this clearance carried out, that the residents of Newhaven soon began to pour in the complaints. The explosives used had caused windows of houses in the town to smash, along with other damage, that naturally the disposal work was brought to a rapid halt! Today the wreckage is broken up and lying in three main parts, though in only about 10 metres of water.

The *Ocean Sunlight* was not the only naval vessel to sink after hitting a mine off Newhaven. Four weeks later, on the 17th July, a cable layer suffered the same fate as the minesweeper. Once more the *Cecil & Lilian Philpott* was launched, only to be beaten again to the sinking vessel, though this time by a naval patrol boat. It was this

SELSEY LIFEBOAT R.N.L.B. CANADIAN PACIFIC [BY KIND PERMISSION OF THE R.N.L.I.]

boat that picked up the survivors. Nevertheless, the lifeboat crew were still rewarded - this time the sum of £5 5s.

All manner of naval craft were to request the help of the R.N.L.I. whilst at sea off the Sussex Coast. For example, on the 22nd November 1941, it was the turn of a naval patrol boat. At 7.05pm the N.O.I.C. at Newhaven requested the services of a lifeboat for the patrol vessel *H.M.S. Joseph* that was in difficulties near the harbour entrance. The *Joseph*, stationed at Dover, had in fact run aground in the shelter off the breakwater. So at 7.30 the *Cecil & Lilian Philpott* was launched, coming alongside the *Joseph* minutes later. Despite the best efforts of the strong tide the lifeboat crew succeeded in re-floating the *Joseph* and her 12 crew. The patrol boat was escorted back into the harbour at 11.45pm, the lifeboat crew receiving the grateful thanks of the N.O.I.C.

Perhaps it was a consequence of their design or shallow draught, that a number of naval lifting craft were to provide work for the R.N.L.I. On the 2nd February 1945 it was the turn of the Selsey lifeboat, the *Canadian Pacific*, to assist the navy. Just after midday the naval authorities at Portsmouth reported that a floating crane was in trouble in Hayling Bay. This was no doubt the effect of a south-west gale and a rough sea. Having been launched at 1.35pm, the *Canadian Pacific* found the crane dragging its anchor and drifting out of control towards Chichester Harbour. Nearby was a tug, the *LT.639*, but she was unable to get close enough to render any assistance.

A plan was devised whereby the lifeboat crew transferred a rope from the tug to the crew on the crane. Once the lifeboat crew had successfully achieved this, with their usual expertise, the crane was taken in tow by the tug. The lifeboat finally stood down in Hayling Bay at 3.40pm, returning to Selsey at 5.50pm.

An almost identical rescue had been completed three years earlier on the 3rd September 1942. Once again it was the Newhaven lifeboat that was involved. Lifting barge *No. 17*, on salvage work near Newhaven, had broken free from her moorings near the harbour mouth at about 3pm. Again this was the result of rough conditions and a strong south-west wind. Launched at 3.15pm, the *Cecil & Lilian Philpott* managed to pass a rope from the crane across to a waiting tug. They in turn towed the crane into the safety of the harbour, with the lifeboat standing by throughout.

Another naval vessel that required the services of the Newhaven lifeboat was *H.M.S. Supporter*. She was an Admiralty drifter that had been converted into a hospital carrier. At 9.10pm on the evening of the 3rd November 1944 the N.O.I.C. at Newhaven reported that the *Supporter*, which since D-Day had been busy between the Normandy beaches and the south coast, was getting into difficulties near the harbour. Fifty-five minutes later the *Cecil & Lilian Philpott* was launched into a choppy sea. Just before she had set out, the lifeboat's crew asked the skipper of a nearby naval vessel if they could supply a signaller, as their usual crewman was unavailable. As he could not supply a signaller from his own crew, Lieut-Commander E.C. Hoblyn R.N.V.R. left his bunk and volunteered himself to the lifeboat! As soon as the lifeboat pulled away from the harbour mouth they found the *Supporter*. She had gone ashore on the beach east of the eastern harbour arm, and was taking water badly. Pulling alongside, the lifeboat safely removed the crew of 12 and returned them to the shore. Throughout the following night, the *Supporter* was gradually broken up by the extremely rough seas.

THEY ALSO SERVED

NEWHAVEN LIFEBOAT **R.N.L.B. CECIL & LILLIAN PHILPOTT** [BY KIND PERMISSION OF THE R.N.L.I.]

It was not only vessels of the Royal Navy that called on the services of the R.N.L.I, as an incident on the 16th August 1940 shows. At 1pm the Selsey lifeboat had put to sea following reports from the coastguard of at least four aircraft in the sea four miles west of Selsey Bill - the Battle of Britain was at its height. The *Canadian Pacific* arrived at the scene to find that a high-speed launch of the R.A.F. was already present, and in fact had already rescued two German airmen.

These men were in fact the crew of a Junkers Ju87 dive-bomber from the 3rd Staffel KG2. They had been part of a force of dive-bombers that had attacked the RAF fighter base at Tangmere. During the raid they were intercepted by Hurricane fighters of No.43 and No.601 Squadrons. Fatally hit, the bomber crashed into the channel just before 1pm. Uffz. P. Bohn and Obergefr. J. Bader were able to escape before the aircraft sank.

Seeing the two airmen safe onboard the R.A.F. launch, the lifeboat crew continued the search. Finding nothing, the lifeboat turned and began to head for home. On route they saw an air-sea rescue seaplane on the water about three miles further east. The plane was signalling frantically, requesting the help of the lifeboat. On reaching the aircraft, the *Canadian Pacific* found that the R.A.F. launch was now stranded - a length of rope having fouled its propeller. At this point the lifeboat crew spotted the bodies of two other German airmen in the water. They were picked up and transferred to the seaplane which then lifted off and headed back towards Shoreham. As for the R.A.F. launch, this was taken in tow by the lifeboat and returned to harbour.

By the 21st of March 1945 the war in Europe was almost at an end, but nevertheless this was the day on which an R.A.F. salvage vessel, the *Dutch Lady*, required the services of the Shoreham lifeboat. At 5.18pm the coastguard reported that the *Dutch Lady* was off Goring and leaking badly. Despite a thick fog the *Rosa Woodd & Phyllis Lunn* was underway by 5.48pm. On arrival the lifeboat crew found that the R.A.F. vessel was taking water, but still able to proceed under her own steam. It was decided that the salvage boat should head for Littlehampton with the lifeboat escorting her. This difficult and painfully slow passage was finally completed by 11.05pm when the lifeboat was able to stand down.

LANDING CRAFT AND D-DAY

It was early in 1943, some sixteen months before the Normandy landings, that the mysterious initials 'L.C.' first appeared in a report to the Institution headquarters, from one of its stations. A vast number of these 'L.C.', or landing craft, were specifically built for the impending invasion of Europe, and many were moving around the British coast, participating in exercises or positioning themselves at various ports. The first call to a landing craft was at Peterhead in Aberdeenshire, where a LCT, (Landing Craft Tank), had run aground on rocks.

Some months later in April 1944, as invasion preparations were well advanced, the R.N.L.I. offered its lifeboats to the Admiralty. In return the Naval Authorities asked that up to fifteen boats be made available between The Wash and The Bristol Channel. The boats and their crews were made ready, but as D-Day passed the call was never made. Despite this, for some time before D-Day the lifeboats, including those in Sussex, were still actively engaged in assisting the landing craft that were frequently getting into difficulty. In June 1944 over 80 men were saved from landing craft in these launches.

After D-Day the lifeboats continued to assist landing craft, but also the giant sections of the Mulberry Harbours that got into difficulty during their passage across the Channel. An example is the Appledore lifeboat, which chased a caisson that had gone adrift for thirty miles. In poor weather all its crew were rescued.

LANDING CRAFT **LCT2014** ON THE SLIPWAY AT GOLF-COURSE BEACH LITTLEHAMPTON [BY KIND PERMISSION OF MARY TAYLOR]

THEY ALSO SERVED

There are many examples of the Sussex lifeboats assisting landing craft in difficulty, but nearly all occurred after the D-Day landings. One of the first involved the Shoreham lifeboat, the *Rosa Woodd &Phyllis Lunn*, on the 24th January 1944. Here assistance was given to the landing craft *LCV 42*, (landing craft vehicle), when she got into difficulty off Shoreham.

On the 10th July 1944 the Shoreham lifeboat was again called out, though this time for the *LCT 37-940*. At 1.55 in the afternoon a message was sent from the coastguard stating that a landing craft had broken down some six miles south-south-west of Shoreham harbour. As there was a heavy swell with a strong south-west wind blowing, the landing craft, without any engines, quickly got into difficulty. She began to drift out of control towards the shore. Her crew, working frantically, managed to carry out repairs and soon the vessel was able to make her way once again.

Despite the fact that the coastguard in a second message reported this, the Naval Authorities, in consultation with the honorary secretary, asked that the *Rosa Woodd & Phyllis Lunn* be launched. This was done at 3.14pm. When the lifeboat reached the landing craft, she took up station alongside and remained there until the arrival of a tug from Shoreham. The L.C.T. was taken in tow back to Shoreham, followed by the lifeboat, which returned to her station at 5.45pm.

Nearly six months later, in the early hours of the 5th November 1944, the *Rosa Woodd & Phyllis Lunn*, was in action once more. At 2.12am it was reported that the *LCT.532* was offshore and signalling for help. Her diesel tank had been damaged and her fuel stock lost. At this point the Naval Authorities said that the Shoreham Harbour tug was out of action, and asked that a lifeboat be sent. So with her crew mustered, the Shoreham lifeboat was launched at 2.50am.

At 3.55am she found the stricken landing craft seven miles south-east of the harbour. A south-west gale was blowing and there was a very heavy swell. In such conditions and with the landing craft being so large, (*LCT.532* being designed to transport tanks), all the lifeboat could do was stand alongside in case the naval crew should need to be taken off. Helpless, the LCT drifted out of control until, at 7.15am, the Newhaven tug finally arrived. At last LCT.532 was taken in tow and, with the lifeboat still in attendance, made for the safety of Newhaven. With the weather still unfavourable, the journey took until 10.59am to complete, at which point the *Rosa Woodd & Phyllis Lunn* was released and

Launching of Hastings Lifeboat R.N.L.B. Cyril & Lillian Bishop [By kind permission of the R.N.L.I.]

allowed to return to her station. For what was a remarkably long duty in appalling conditions, the lifeboat crew were rewarded with the sum of £21 15s.

The Hastings lifeboat carried out a more dramatic rescue nearly two weeks later on the 17th November. At 9.50am the coastguard telephoned a message to the honorary secretary. It stated that a landing craft was in difficulty and struggling in the bad weather between Hastings and Fairlight. A further call seventeen minutes later reported that the vessel was now making distress signals. In fact the landing craft was going ashore between Pett Level and Winchelsea. The conditions were appalling - a very rough sea was being whipped up by a strong southerly gale.

Even before the second message from the coastguard the Hastings lifeboat had been launched at 10am. Immediately the *Cyril & Lilian Bishop* headed for the reported position of the landing craft off Pett. On arrival nothing was seen, for unbeknown to the

THEY ALSO SERVED

lifeboat crew, the landing craft had been forced ashore at Galloways. The 29 strong naval crew had managed to get onto the beach. Not possessing this vital piece of information, the lifeboat continued its search - with almost disastrous consequences.

The conditions at sea failed to improve throughout the continuing search. As the *Cyril & Lilian Bishop* reached a point 2 miles south-west of Rye Harbour the huge swell caused her to capsize. As she turned completely over, three of her crew, one of who was the coxswain, were washed overboard. A fourth crewmember was badly injured, sustaining a broken nose. Thankfully the three washed overboard were able to stay afloat and clung to the capsized hull. The lifeboat was then righted, and surprisingly the engine started on the first attempt. With all the crew back on board, the lifeboat headed back to shore, arriving at her station at 1.10pm.

The lifeboat had been damaged in the rescue and was therefore placed off service. It had been a terrifying ordeal for the crew, and so an increase in the usual rewards was made. To the crew and those helpers on shore (who were twice soaked wet through) the standard reward of £31 5s. was paid. The additional money awarded was £24 14s., a grand total of £55 19s. being paid. The crewman who nose had been broken was also compensated separately.

The 17th November 1944 also saw the Selsey Lifeboat being launched to assist a landing craft. According to the R.N.L.I. records this service was carried out by the reserve vessel the *Hearts of Oak*. It was reported that a landing craft had run aground after getting into difficulty. The lifeboat was launched and reached the vessel some time later. However, on arrival the lifeboat crew found that the tide had fallen, providing the naval crew with the opportunity to walk ashore at low water! This rescue, less dramatic than the one made by the Hastings lifeboat, was in fact one of the last occasions on which a Sussex lifeboat was called to a stricken landing craft.

MEDAL SERVICE

In some of the previous chapters the rescue of several naval vessels has already been described. This chapter, however, concentrates on the services to two other naval vessels - *H.M.S. President Briand* and *H.M.S. Caulonia*. These rescues were different to the others in that they were to become the subject of medal awards to the crews of the lifeboats involved.

Floating at position 50 55 15; 00 50 14 in Rye Bay can be found a beacon with a top mark of two black spheres. This beacon is intended to mark the position of a stranded wreck - the remains of the requisitioned trawler *H.M.S. Caulonia*. Built in 1912, this trawler, weighing some 296 tons and with a crew of 34, sank on the 31st March 1943 when she was just 600 yards south of the coastguard station at Jury's Gap near Camber.

It was at 2.15 in the morning of the 31st that a message arrived from Dover requesting that the Hastings lifeboat be launched and sent to a vessel sinking ten and a half miles from Hastings. The weather was grim. The wind was close to gale force, with heavy rain and a rough sea. Despite such appalling conditions, the launch itself was to prove the greatest problem.

For some time past contractors had been working on the coastal defences at Hastings, and the beach around the lifeboat station was blocked by all manner of objects. Soldiers from nearby batteries assisted, organised by the honorary secretary and the motor mechanic of the lifeboat. With the conditions deteriorating still further, the *Cyril & Lilian Bishop* was finally brought to the water s edge. The launchers and military volunteers put the lifeboat into the water, but a heavy sea coming from a breach in the old harbour threw her back up the beach. Once again the lifeboat was launched, this time successfully. At 4.30am the lifeboat began its battle with the elements to reach Jury's Gap.

With dawn approaching, the wind began to weaken. Thanks to a strong following sea the lifeboat reached the *Caulonia* just after 5.50am. The sea was breaking about a quarter of mile offshore and the lifeboat crew could see that the trawler was well inside this turbulent water. She was in obvious trouble, lying broadside to the waves with her fore part under water. The anti-aircraft gun mounted aft was only just visible. The coastguard

THE RESIDENTS OF HASTINGS FORGET THE WAR FOR ONE DAY AS THEY ENJOY THEIR LIFEBOAT OPEN DAY - NOTE THE ANTI-TANK BLOCKS IN THE BEACH! [BY KIND PERMISSION OF THE R.N.L.I.]

had already fired eight rockets with lines attached from the shore, but only eleven of the crew had managed to get ashore. Seventeen more had taken to a raft, and the remainder were gathered around the base of the ship's funnel.

As they moved closer to the trawler, the lifeboat crew watched in horror as the *Caulonia*'s bridge was swept away. Realising that time was rapidly running out the coxswain ordered the lifeboat to approach around the trawler's stern. However, the heaving seas, floating debris and a strong tide made it almost impossible for the lifeboat to come alongside the stricken vessel. A line was thrown across, and with the engines working hard all the time, the coxswain was finally able to go alongside. Even more spectacular was the fact that the lifeboat, through the very best seamanship, stayed like this for almost thirty minutes. As the last of the remaining crew were taken on board, the Dungeness lifeboat arrived, having also been requested by the naval authorities at Dover, only to find her services no longer required. The final seven members of the trawler's crew were therefore successfully rescued and brought back to shore. The *Cyril & Lilian Bishop* finally returned to her station undamaged, though scratched and battered, at five past eight. The extreme difficulties involved in this particular rescue had resulted in the crew of the lifeboat displaying nothing but the very highest skills and seamanship. The Institution itself recognised this and made a number of awards to the crew.

The coxswain, John Muggridge, and the motor-mechanic, W.R. Hilder, were both awarded the bronze medal for gallantry, along with a copy of the vote on vellum. Sadly though both of these men were never to see these medals. Only days after the rescue John Muggridge was killed when his fishing boat was blown up after hitting a mine. Two months later Hilder was also to lose his life, a victim of a bombing raid on Hastings. The second-coxswain, Edward Adams, and the bowman, Frederick White, along with the honorary secretary, Commander W. Highfield, each received the thanks of the Institution inscribed on vellum. All the crew were given an extra reward of 15s. this being in addition to the standard scale that was normally awarded.

Much earlier in the war, on the 16th November 1941, the Shoreham lifeboat was involved in the rescue of the crew of the minesweeper *President Briand*. Again it was early in the morning, and again the weather was appalling. With her engine working only temperamentally, the minesweeper was in grave danger of being forced aground by the heavy sea. So it was that at about 1am the *Rosa Woodd & Phyllis Lunn* was launched. Coming alongside, the naval captain asked if the lifeboat would wait. The lifeboat crew complied, standing off until 9.30am, when with better conditions and a tug on the way, the lifeboat was able to stand down and return to her station.

The coxswain was then asked to return to the *President Briand* in the pilot-cutter and act as pilot whilst the minesweeper was brought into the harbour. As he was being put on board, the *S.S. Goole*, one of the Shoreham harbour blockships, was ordered out to help with the tow. Things, however, then began to deviate from the plans. The wind began to increase, gusting to gale force at times. Not only was the *President Briand* and her assisting tug now both in danger of being washed ashore, but the *Goole* just narrowly missed being wrecked as she tried to navigate the harbour entrance.

So at 9.45 the *Rosa Woodd & Phyllis Lunn* was launched for the second time. With the coxswain still on board the minesweeper, the second-coxswain assumed command. The lifeboat found the tug desperately trying to pull the minesweeper clear of the shore. The lifeboat took up a towrope, but both ropes simply broke. By now the minesweeper was close inshore and in very shallow water. In a last-ditch attempt to save herself she dropped her anchor, but this simply struck the bottom, lying there completely useless.

The minesweeper began to roll heavily, the heavy seas breaking over her.

The lifeboat, seeing the predicament the naval vessel was now in, moved straight in alongside. By repeating this tricky manoeuvre six or seven times, the entire crew of twenty-one was taken off. The coxswain was also re-united with his vessel! At one stage, the lifeboat's bow had been lifted up onto the minesweeper's rail, damaging her stern. Nevertheless, with the naval crew safely on board, the lifeboat turned for home. As she started to battle her way through the heavy seas, with waves washing across her, the crew looked back just in time to see the *President Briand* heel over on her beam. It was at noon, eleven exhausting hours since first having been called out, that the *Rosa Woodd & Phyllis Lunn* again took up her station at Shoreham.

As was the case with the rescue of the crew of the *Caulonia*, the R.N.L.I. did not allow such a morning s work to pass un-noticed. The Acting-coxswain, James Upperton, was awarded the silver medal for gallantry along with a copy of the vote inscribed on vellum. Henry Philcox, the motor-mechanic, was awarded the bronze medal for gallantry, also receiving a copy of the vote on vellum. To the other five members of the crew, bowman John Laker, assistant motor-mechanic Cecil Ayling, and life-boatmen Albert Upperton, Charles Laker and Victor Page, the Institution sent its thanks inscribed on vellum.

ACTING COXSWAIN JAMES UPPERTON WAS AWARDED THE R.N.L.I'S SILVER MEDAL FOR GALLANTRY DURING THE SRVICE TO THE PRESIDENT BRIAND
[BY KIND PERMISSION OF THE R.N.L.I.]

THE ULTIMATE SACRIFICE

The weather on the evening of the 23rd November 1943 was poor - a gale was blowing and the sea very rough. The night was dark, visibility worse than poor and the rain was relentless. It was a night that one would not have wanted to be at sea.

However, at 8.40pm the N.O.I.C. at Newhaven sent a message to the Newhaven lifeboat, asking that she be made ready to put to sea. The crew were called in, and by 9pm the honorary secretary was able to send the reply that the *Cecil & Lilian Philpott* was standing by. With the crew assembled, time slowly slipped by until, at 9.42pm, the N.O.I.C. requested that the lifeboat be launched. Because no other information had been forthcoming, the honorary secretary asked the position to which the lifeboat was to go and what service was expected of her. The N.O.I.C. supplied a location some two miles from Newhaven, and it was to here that the lifeboat headed when she put to sea at 9.45pm.

When the position was reached, the lifeboat's crew were unable to find anything. The shore signal station was sending out messages, but the appalling conditions meant that the crew were unable to read them. As a result the coxswain made the decision to return the lifeboat to her station. As they approached the harbour mouth, a signal was received instructing the lifeboat to now make for a position east of Newhaven.

The *Cecil & Lilian Philpott* headed some four or five miles east of the harbour, where near the mouth of the River Cuckmere, at Hope Gap, the crew saw the lights of a vessel. She was firing rockets, red green and white, and burning flares. Searchlights from a nearby shore battery were playing on the water, but their dazzling light proved more of a hindrance to the lifeboat crew than a help. Despite the weather, the coxswain could make out a large trawler. She was in fact *H.M.S. Avanturine*, a pre-war trawler requisitioned by the admiralty for naval service. The *Avanturine*, with a crew of 25 on board, was in extreme danger. She was only 200 to 300 yards off the rocky shoreline and, as the coxswain immediately realised, even closer to a reef that was capable of holing her port beam.

The coxswain decided that the only thing they could do was to anchor, drop down on his cable with the wind and tide, and go under the trawler's lee side. He let go the anchor,

THE EXTENT OF THE DAMAGE TO THE CECIL & LILIAN PHILPOTT CAN CLEARLY BE SEEN IN THIS PHOTOGRAPH [BY KIND PERMISSION OF THE R.N.L.I.]

and had run out about forty fathoms of cable when suddenly, out of the darkness, the *Avanturine*, thought to have been at anchor, appeared close to the lifeboat coming at her with full speed. The coxswain put his engines full astern, but it was too late. As the trawler was lifted out of a trough by the heavy seas, the lifeboat was washed forward crashing against the *Avanturine*'s bow. It cut right through the lifeboat's side, water pouring in. The mast had been broken into three pieces and was washed overboard taking the wireless set with it. Five of the crew had been knocked off their feet.

The Coxswain knew that the *Cecil & Lilian Philpott* had been badly damaged, but how bad he did not yet know. The boat was at once put astern, and orders given for the anchor to be taken in and stowed. What remained of the mast and rigging was cleared from the deck. As the crew struggled to carry out these commands the coxswain noticed a large wave approaching the boat and shouted 'hold on' to his colleagues. As it hit the lifeboat, water raged across the open deck, taking with it one of the crew - the bowman and signalman, Benjamin J. Clark.

The coxswain himself had been flung heavily against the wheel and was suffering intense pain in his back. Three other crewmembers had been injured, leaving only one uninjured man on deck. The two motor-mechanics had also escaped injury. By now the lifeboat was becoming increasingly hard to steer, and the petrol tank hatch had been washed overboard, leaving a large open space on the deck creating yet another hazard for the crew in the darkness. Worse still, there had been no further sign of Benjamin Clark.

In spite of this the coxswain and crew of the lifeboat continued with their duty. They eventually found the *Avanturine*, which had steamed off, once again. The lifeboat escorted the trawler to a position some two or three miles from the harbour entrance. Here the trawler could anchor safely for the remainder of the night. With the wireless set and its operator both lost, the lifeboat was unable to communicate with the shore and receive further instructions. The coxswain had the lifeboat standby offshore to see if there were any other signs of vessels in difficulty. As nothing else was seen in the horrible conditions, the lifeboat began to head for home. This, though, was to be no simple task.

The hole that had been ripped in the side of the lifeboat was on the weatherside, water still pouring in. Control and steering were becoming almost impossible. This, and the pain that the coxswain was now suffering, taxed his skill and strength to the utmost. Thankfully the crew were eventually able to bring the lifeboat safely home, berthing at half past midnight, some one and a half hours after having collided with the *Avanturine*.

A naval surgeon had been waiting for the crew to return, and he immediately set about tending their wounds. The coxswain had a badly bruised back. The second coxswain had injuries to his eyes and the bridge of his nose. His body and legs were covered in bruises. One of the other crewmembers had lost his false teeth, which had been smashed to pieces in his mouth. His bottom lip required stitches, which was done by the naval surgeon, and he also had sustained wounds to his hands, arms, head and chest - all being heavily bruised. A fourth crewman was suffering from bruises and cuts. Once treated, all the injured men were taken home by naval transport arranged by the N.O.I.C. at Newhaven.

The missing crewman was not forgotten. Throughout the following day patrols were sent out along the beaches east and west of Newhaven. Coastguard, Navy and Army personnel continued the search for Benjamin Clark until, at midday, his body was found washed ashore east from Newhaven. Benjamin Clark had been 49 years old at the time of his death, and had been a crewmember of the Newhaven lifeboats for some 25 years. Both his father and brother also had long records of service with the Institution, both serving as coxswain. At the inquest into his death, which took place on the 26th November 1943, a verdict of accidental drowning was recorded. As was his own wish, Benjamin Clark was buried at sea. The arrangements and costs were both taken care of by the R.N.L.I. He left a widow, and the Institution pensioned her from the day of his death, as if Clark had been a sailor, soldier or airman who had been killed in action. The

Navy organised a collection, raising £40 for the benefit of his widow. As well as compensating the injured crewmen for the time they were unable to work after the incident, the Institution also made the following awards in recognition of the gallantry and endurance shown by the crew despite their injuries and the damage suffered by the *Cecil & Lilian Philpott*.

Benjamin Clark was posthumously awarded the bronze medal for gallantry, and his widow received a certificate recording his devotion to duty and the sacrifice he made. The coxswain, Leonard Peddlesden, was awarded the silver medal for gallantry with a copy of the vote inscribed on vellum. The second-coxswain Frederick Parker; the motor-mechanic R. Lower; the acting assistant motor-mechanic J. Eager; and lifeboatmen S. Winter, S. Holden and H. Moore were awarded the bronze medal for gallantry and copies of the vote inscribed on vellum.

As well as the medal awards, the R.N.L.I. also presented the honorary secretary with an inscribed barometer. The head launcher, R. Holden, received a letter of thanks, and similar letters were also sent to the naval authorities at Newhaven and Mr Cardy, the divisional marine manager of the Southern Railway, for their help with the burial at sea.

As for the *Cecil & Lilian Philpott*, in the calm of day it was found that she had been severely damaged. The heavy seas had driven the stern of the *Avanturine* two feet into

TWO DAYS AFTER THE LOSS OF BENJAMIN CLARK, THE SURVIVNG CREW OF NEWHAVEN LIFEBOAT ARE ON THE ROAD TO RECOVERY [BY KIND PERMISSION OF THE R.N.L.I.]

THEY ALSO SERVED

the hull of the lifeboat. A hole had been ripped into the side just abaft the port shoulder, from the deck to the bilge keel. The hole was some 5' from top to bottom, and 2'6" at the widest point. The port petrol tank had been bulked, and in the process was driven against a bulkhead with such violence that the bulkhead itself was fractured. This had allowed water to pour into the after holds and the cabin.

In fact, it was this damage that had caused the lifeboat to become unwieldy and difficult to steer. Thankfully, although the petrol tank had been moved off its seating and badly buckled, it had not been punctured. This allowed the engine to continue working, without failure, until the lifeboat finally returned home. A patch was put over the hole, and on the 30th November, the *Cecil & Lilian Philpott* put to sea again for the first time since the tragedy. She made her way to Shoreham Harbour so that repairs could be made. On the same day a lifeboat from the reserve fleet took up station at Newhaven - ensuring there was no break in coverage by the Institution. The repairs to the lifeboat took four months to complete, at a cost of £650.

This was not the last involvement of the R.N.L.I. with *H.M.S. Avanturine*. At 4.30am on the following morning, the 24th November, the Institution received a report that the trawler was once more in difficulty. Left at anchor off Newhaven, the trawler was again succumbing to the heavy seas and had started dragging her anchor. Unable to despatch the badly damaged *Cecil & Lilian Philpott*, at 5am the *Rosa Woodd & Phyllis Lunn* was launched from Shoreham.

At 7.15am the lifeboat came alongside the trawler. Her crew did not wish to be taken off, but requested that the lifeboat stand to nearby whilst a tug was sent. When the tug finally arrived from Newhaven, the lifeboat escorted the *Avanturine*, which was under tow, into Newhaven. They arrived there at 12.28pm, the lifeboat returning to Shoreham at 6pm having been at sea for thirteen hours. As well as the normal rewards paid, an extra sum of £1 was given to the coxswain and seven other crewmembers of the *Rosa Woodd & Phyllis Lunn*.

Benjamin Clark was to be the only lifeboatman to lose his life in the waters of Sussex for the duration of the war. He was, and still is, the perfect example of the people who crew our lifeboats, willing to risk their life to save others in peril.

On this occasion however, Benjamin Clark made the ultimate sacrifice.

THEY ALSO SERVED

YACHTS AND OTHER MATTERS

Even in times of war the daily life of the Channel and our coastline went on, changed and diminished, but still recognisable. There were still people who got into difficulty bathing, people cut off by the tides or people who climbed down cliffs only to become stranded. More unusual though, was the flotsam of war. Lifeboats brought ashore all manner of items - a meteorological balloon, a paravane that had broken free from a minesweeper, oxygen bottles, aircraft fuel tanks or even airmen's gloves.

It was on the 22nd December 1943 that the Eastbourne lifeboat experienced first hand the flotsam of war. The *Jane Holland* had been called out by the naval authorities and tasked to search an area of the Channel in Pevensey Bay. All that the crew found were two floats, each about four foot long, drifting on the tide. Unsure of what the objects were, the crew decided to leave them alone, mindful of the fact that they could well contain explosives!

The Hastings lifeboat had received a similar call on the 19th August 1942. A coastguard observer at Fairlight reported seeing what he thought was a rubber dinghy fall from a passing aircraft. The time was 11.30am, and the plane has been seen flying west to east. Initially the coastguard tried to contact the air-sea rescue services, but this was to prove unsuccessful. As a result, at 12.22pm, the *Cyril & Lilian Bishop* was launched.

A PARVANE FROM A MINESWEEPER IS RECOVERED AND BEACHED BY HASTINGS LIFEBOAT [BY KIND PERMISSION OF THE R.N.L.I.]

There was a shortage of launchers causing a fear that the lifeboat might not be able to put to sea. However this situation was thankfully resolved by the timely arrival of some 25 soldiers from a nearby shore battery who offered their assistance. Once launched, the lifeboat headed through a slight swell to the position reported by the coastguard - one and a quarter miles south-south-west of Hastings. Almost before reaching this spot the crew came across and recovered an aircraft's petrol tank. The lifeboat then began a sweep of the area concerned, during which another object was spotted to the westward. When they pulled alongside, the crew found that it was a paravane that had probably come adrift from a passing minesweeper. This was taken in tow and returned to the shore at 1.15pm.

Many of the rescues in which lifeboats assisted were unique, though perhaps none were stranger than one such incident to which the New Brighton lifeboat was sent. Though not a Sussex lifeboat, this story is still worthy of mention. This was not a call to assist a stricken boat, but three motor vehicles. Three ambulances from an American Hospital Unit were being used in exercises on the sands at the mouth of the River Mersey. One of the ambulances was driven into a soft patch of sand and promptly became stuck. A tow truck and a repair truck were sent to assist, but they simply suffered the same fate. As the five soldiers involved pondered the next step, the tide slowly but surely advanced. The troops continued their struggle unaware that the tide was closing in around them. Suddenly they realised their predicament - two swimming ashore. The other three, unable to swim, took refuge on the top of the trucks. The New Brighton lifeboat was called to assist and made for the scene with all haste. It arrived just in the nick of time. Two of the soldiers were standing on the roof of the ambulance, whilst the third was clinging to the crane of the tow truck, with only his head showing above the rising tide!

On the 8th August 1940, the Shoreham lifeboat was also called to a strange rescue. At 3.20pm the Beach Manager at Brighton reported, via the coastguard, that a number of men were marooned on the far end of the Palace Pier at Brighton. They were unable to get back to the shore as the military had demolished the centre part of the pier as an anti-invasion measure. The *Rosa Woodd & Phyllis Lunn* was subsequently launched at 4.50pm. The honorary secretary, Captain C.T. Keigwin R.N.R., and an armed guard were on board. On arrival at the south end of the pier, the lifeboat crew were confronted by no fewer than 29 stranded men. With considerable difficulty and at some risk, courtesy of a rough sea and heavy swell, the men were all taken on board the lifeboat. They were all safely landed in Shoreham Harbour at 5.50pm. For their work, the Brighton Corporation sent the R.N.L.I a donation.

Another rescue involving stranded persons took place near Hastings on the 24th March 1944. Two young boys, aged 10 and 12, had been playing on the beaches to the east of the town when they had become trapped by the incoming tide. It was about 11am when a local fisherman, out on his own in a rowing dinghy, saw the boys trapped under the cliffs some 50 yards west of Ecclesbourne Glen. As he got closer he realised that they were stranded on a rock outcrop, unable to reach the beach again, and in danger of drowning as the tide continued to rise.

The fisherman called on a nearby fishing boat, the *RX.47*, to stand by. He then made his approach to the outcrop and successfully lifted the boys into his dinghy. He then made his way back to the *RX.47*. Its two crew took the dinghy in tow and made for the safety of Hastings. The R.N.L.I. rewarded the fisherman 10s., whilst the crew of the *RX.47* received 15s. with 2s. 6d. for the fuel that had been used.

Many of the calls to which Sussex lifeboats were sent provided the crews with a reminder of the pre-war rescues. Such was the case on Sunday the 10th of September 1939. The coastguard reported that the sailing yacht *Wisp*, of Shoreham, had capsized about one and a half miles from the harbour entrance. The sea was rough, with a strong westerly wind blowing. Nevertheless, the *Rosa Woodd & Phyllis Lunn* was launched at 5.21pm.

Arriving shortly after, the lifeboat crew rescued the two people who had been on board the *Wisp*. Both were exhausted and suffering from the effects of the cold water. With the yacht s crew safe, the *Wisp* was taken in tow and returned to her homeport at 6.10pm.

It was in the very last days of the war, on the 26th April 1945, that the *Rosa Woodd & Phyllis Lunn* was again to taste a reminder of its pre-war work. At 2.55am a message was received that there was a boat adrift west of Worthing Pier and that there had been no reply to signals made from the shore. As no boats or crew were available at Worthing, it was asked if the Shoreham lifeboat could be launched. This was done at 3.35am, pitching her into a calm sea and light breeze. About a mile south-west of the pier, the lifeboat crew recovered the drifting boat. No one was on board and she was awash. With the boat in tow the lifeboat headed back for her station, arriving at 5.35 that morning.

Even when not manning their lifeboats, R.N.L.I. crewmembers were never far from danger throughout the war years. This was particularly the case for those stationed on the South Coast with its close proximity to occupied Europe. The coxswain of the Hastings lifeboat, for example, was sadly killed in his own fishing boat when it was destroyed by a mine. Three men from the Eastbourne lifeboat crew nearly suffered a similar fate. They were out fishing in their own boat, when a German aeroplane attacked them. The boat was riddled from end to end by machine-gun fire. All three men were wounded, and one man in particular had fourteen splinters removed from his shoulder.

The risk of death or injury did not necessarily arise from an aerial attack. On the 29th July 1940 a trawler at work off Brighton struck a mine. The resulting explosion was so great that the boat sank immediately and almost without trace. The Shoreham lifeboat, the *Rosa Woodd & Phyllis Lunn*, was launched and raced to the scene. Despite an extensive search of the location given by the coastguard, no trace of the trawler was ever found.

It was at 1.18pm on the 17th May 1942 that the Hastings lifeboat received a message that a local fishing boat was in trouble about one and a half miles south-east of the harbour at Hastings. In fact the fishing boat *Good Luck* had been the subject of a machine-gun attack by a passing German aircraft. Despite the fact that an air raid was under way onshore, the coxswain of the *Cyril & Lillian Bishop* and four other men put to sea in another motorboat. They came across the *Good Luck* half a mile out, and escorted her back towards the shore and into harbour. No one on board the *Good Luck* had been wounded, though the boat herself was badly holed and taking in water. For their work, the coxswain and his four crew were rewarded £3 2s. 6d.

There was, however, one vital part of the R.N.L.I. that was not changed by the outset of war - the question of fund raising. Even in those grim years the R.N.L.I. needed to collect the donations with which it could operate. Rescued crews and grateful ship owners still made donations, but in the usual tradition different methods were still being invented in an attempt to get the British public to part with it's money! Neither the destruction of war, increasing taxation or the other demands on the purses of the British people had made them less ready to give to their lifeboat service.

It was in Eastbourne that one different approach was used. It was on the Eastbourne lifeboat day in September 1941 that the 'pennies race' was devised. A stretch of road was set aside by the Chief Constable, and here a race took place between two teams.

The first was led by the Mayor, leading a team of six ladies from the Women's Auxiliary Air Force, whilst the second, led by the Mayoress, consisted of six men from the Royal Air Force.

The teams started at opposing ends of the stretch of road and began to work towards the middle. As they went they asked the watching public for money, and it was laid along the kerbstones at a rate of thirty pennies to a yard. The course was some 118 yards long, and the first team that reached the middle were declared the winners! In 1941, the team from the R.A.F. won by two yards, covering their half in just over one hour. In the course of this race £14 15s. was raised for the R.N.L.I.

The 1941 'pennies race' proved such a success that it was to be repeated in the next two years. 1942 saw the amount raised climb to just over £60. In 1943 however, some ten teams took part, among them being groups from the R.A.F., the W.A.A.F., the Air Training Corps, the Naval Cadets, the National Fire Service, various Civil Defence departments and the Eastbourne Police. As a result 1943 proved the beat fundraiser yet, with the sum of £73 raised. The Eastbourne Police were declared the winners.

Whilst such events not only provided fun in times of seriousness, they also helped ensure that the lifeboat service was able to carry on its great tradition, whether war or peace reigned, and that in so doing was still able to save the lives of those at peril on the seas around our shores.

EVEN DURING THE WAR THE **R.N.L.I.** STILL NEEDED TO RAISE FUNDS FOR ITS LIFEBOATS. EASTBOURNE'S 'PENNIES RACE' WAS A CROWD PLEASER WITH THE **RAF** WINNING THE FIRST RACE IN **1941** - BY **1943** IT WAS THE TURN OF THE LOCAL POLICE TO TAKE THE HONOURS [BY KIND PERMISSION OF THE R.N.L.I.]

THEY ALSO SERVED

THE SERVICE LIST

Please note that in the following list the presence of a* alongside a date Indicates rewards paid by RNLI, but no involvement of a lifeboat or shore boat. If a date is marked with bold type and italics this means that the incident is described in further detail within the book.

DATE	LIFEBOAT	SERVICE	CONCLUSION
1939			
09.09.39	*Hastings*	*Avro Anson ditched one mile east of Fairlight.*	*Crew rescued by private boat but aircraft towed ashore*
10.09.39	*Shoreham*	*Sailing yacht Wisp capsized.*	*2 rescued and yacht towed to Shoreham harbour.*
25.09.39	Hastings	Aeroplane reported to have crashed between Hastings and Le Treport.	Area searched by lifeboat and aircraft. Nothing found.
18.10.39	Shoreham	Aircraft reported to have fallen into sea.	Area searched but nothing was found.
20.10.39	*Selsey and Shoreham*	*A Naval aircraft crashed into sea.*	*Lifeboat had engine failure and ran aground. Plane crew swam ashore.*
21.10.39	Shoreham	Emergency flares reported south of Brighton.	Area searched but nothing was found.
13.11.39	Hastings	Fishing vessel Sea Queen from Hastings in difficulty.	Crew of two and vessel saved and escorted to safety.
15.11.39	Selsey	Boat reported floating out to sea.	Found a ship's boat belonging to S.S. Alaska of Le Havre.
03.12.39	Shoreham	Fishing boat Skylark in difficulty.	Crew of three saved and boat escorted to shore.
06.12.39	Shoreham	Fishing boat Skylark again in difficulty.	Vessel escorted to safety.
1940			
04.01.40	Eastbourne	Trawler Georges Edouard of Ostend in difficulty.	Lifeboat crew gave help and stood by.
05.01.40	Shoreham	Motor Vessel Ben Oliver in difficulty.	Crew of five saved and boat escorted to harbour.
08.01.40	Eastbourne	Fishing vessel Monte Carlo of Ostend in difficulty.	Crew of 6 and boat assisted to safety.
10.01.40	Shoreham	Royal Navy aircraft K4627 in trouble.	Assisted by lifeboat.
29.01.40	Selsey	H.M. Trawler Stella Sirius in difficulty.	Assistance given and boat seen to safety.

THEY ALSO SERVED

09.02.40	Hastings	Fishing vessel Venus from Rye in difficulty.	Crew of 3 and the boat saved and escorted to safety.
17.02.40	Newhaven	Barge Veravia in difficulty near harbour mouth.	Escorted to safety.
02.03.40	Newhaven	S.S. Domala bombed by aircraft in Channel.	51 survivors rescued from the S.S. Jonge Willem.
20.03.40	*Eastbourne, Hastings & Newhaven.*	*S.S. Barnhill attacked by German aircraft.*	*Crew rescued, and Barnhill beached.*
29.05.40	Shoreham	Aeroplane reported in sea south-east of harbour.	Area searched but nothing was found.
04.06.40	Selsey	Aircraft crashed south-west of Hayling Island.	Four crew rescued by Bembridge lifeboat, Selsey lifeboat recalled.
11.06.40	*Newhaven*	*St. Ronaig hit mine and sunk*	*2 bodies recovered along with four survivors. 2 missing*
13.06.40	*Newhaven*	*HMS Ocean Sunlight struck mine outside harbour.*	*Crew already rescued, lifeboat crew salvaged equipment.*
02.07.40	Shoreham	Naval Patrol Vessel Montego Bay in difficulty.	Escorted to safety.
09.07.40	Selsey	Aircraft reported down five miles south of Selsey Bill.	Area searched but nothing was found.
11.07.40	*Selsey*	*British aircraft crashed south of Selsey Bill.*	*Pilot rescued and brought ashore.*
13.07.40	*Hastings*	*Lifeboats seen floating at sea*	*Lifeboat made three trips and recovered three lifeboats.*
14.07.40	Shoreham	Aeroplane seen to crash south of Saltdean.	Wreckage found and three bodies recovered.
17.07.40	*Newhaven*	*Cable layer struck sea mine.*	*Crew rescued by Naval patrol boat.*
19.07.40	Shoreham	German aircraft reported to have fallen into sea.	Area searched but nothing was found.
19.07.40	Selsey	German aircraft came down in sea off Aldwick.	No crew found, but wreckage and oil patch seen.
19.07.40	Shoreham	R.A.F. Fighter crashed off coast at Littlehampton.	Pilot swam ashore and lifeboat recalled.
20.07.40	Selsey	British aeroplane reported in the sea 15 miles south of Bognor.	Area searched but nothing was found.
23.07.40	Shoreham	German aircraft crashed in sea	Lifeboat recalled as pilot was rescued by RN Patrol boat.

THEY ALSO SERVED

26.07.40	Shoreham	S.S. Lulonga torpedoed WSW of Shoreham Harbour.	No survivors from Lulonga were found, but 13 from S.S. Broadhurst and 12 from S.S. London Trader were picked up from Lifeboats.
29.07.40	Shoreham	Motor Trawler blown up by enemy mine.	Area searched but nothing was found.
08.08.40	Shoreham	Emergency flares seen at sea.	Crew assembled, but lifeboat did not put to sea.
08.08.40	Shoreham	People stranded on end of the Palace Pier, Brighton.	29 men taken off by boat and landed at Shoreham harbour.
16.08.40	Selsey	Several aeroplanes crashed into sea west of Selsey Bill.	Assisted naval launch in rescue of two crewmen, recovered two bodies and assisted a disabled naval rescue boat.
18.08.40	Selsey	Five aircraft reported to have crashed into sea.	Two wounded German airmen rescued and handed over to the military authorities.
25.08.40	Hastings	German aircraft reported down off Ecclesbourne Glen.	German airman picked up from the water.
05.09.40	Hastings	German aeroplane shot down several miles south of Hastings.	One German pilot rescued.
27.09.40	Hastings	German aircraft crashed one mile south-west of St. Leonards.	Badly injured crew member rescued.
30.09.40	Selsey	Aircraft reported down in sea south-west of Selsey Bill.	One body recovered by the lifeboat.
22.10.40	Hastings	Aircraft was reported to have crashed off Hastings.	Wreckage seen and one crewman rescued.
29.10.40	Selsey	British aircraft reported crashed into sea off Selsey Bill.	Crew saved.
12.11.40	Shoreham	Royal navy examination vessel in difficulty.	Gave help and escorted vessel to safety.
17.11.40	Newhaven	Admiralty Patrol Boat in trouble near harbour.	Escorted to safety.
07.12.40	Hastings	Salvage crew on board the S.S. Barnhill in difficulty.	Two men rescued.
1941			
17.05.41	Shoreham	S.S. Ala bombed by aircraft.	Lifeboatmen put onto Ala and assisted with salvage.
21.06.41	Hastings (Shore boat)	Report of aircraft about to ditch in Channel.	Crew stood by, but later released as not required.
13.07.41	Hastings	Fishing vessels Two Pals and Boy Ben in trouble	Both vessels escorted safely to shore.
27.07.41	Bexhill	British fighter plane crashed	Pilot rescued and brought ashore.

THEY ALSO SERVED

		(Shore boat)	into sea.	
13.08.41	Eastbourne	Salvage party in difficulty on board the S.S. Barnhill.	Seven men rescued.
16.11.41	Shoreham	HMS President Briand in difficulty.	21 crew members saved, but vessel lost.
22.11.41	Newhaven	Patrol Boat Joseph run aground near harbour.	Patrol Boat refloated and escorted into harbour.

1942

04.01.42	Eastbourne	Spitfire seen to crash into sea	Lifeboat recalled as pilot had drowned.
17.05.42	Hastings	S.S. Good Luck machine gunned.	Boat taking water, and escorted to harbour.
19.08.42	Hastings	Dingy seen by coastguard.	Area searched and equipment salvaged.
02.09.42	Hastings	Parachute reported twelve miles south of Hastings.	No bodies found, but wreckage seen.
03.09.42	Newhaven	Lifting craft broken loose from moorings.	Towed to shore by tug, lifeboat assisted.
03.09.42	Newhaven	Admiralty lighter LC17 in trouble near harbour.	Gave help and escorted to safety.
07.12.42	Shoreham	Red flares seen at sea.	Wreckage of British bomber found. Three of crew rescued

1943

31.03.43	Hastings	HMS Caulonia run aground at Jury's Gap.	Seven men rescued by the lifeboat.
11.04.43	Shoreham	S.S. Frode mined whilst in convoy.	One body recovered and crew rescued by other boats.
09.08.43	Eastbourne	British aircraft reported to have crashed in sea.	Area searched and a dinghy was salvaged.
11.08.43	Eastbourne	Aircraft seen to crash in Pevensey Bay.	Dingy recovered by the lifeboat and the crew by RAF launch.
11.08.43	Selsey	British bomber crashed into sea half a mile from coast.	Parachutes recovered by lifeboat and crew by rescue launch.
29.08.43	Shoreham	Landing craft in difficulty in heavy seas.	Help given and landing craft escorted.
06.09.43	Hastings, Eastbourne, Pevensey & Bexhill (Shore Boats).	Bomber aircraft crashed into the sea.	Crew rescued by the shore boats and wreckage seen by the lifeboats.
03.11.43	Newhaven	HMS Supporter in difficulties	HMS Supporter ran aground, but 12 crew rescued.

outside harbour.

03.11.43	Hastings	S.S. Foam Queen in difficulty off coast.	Assistance given by lifeboat and crew.
23.11.43	*Newhaven*	*H.M. Trawler Avanturine in difficulty in heavy seas.*	*Trawler found and escorted to safety.*
24.11.43	*Shoreham*	*H.M. Trawler Avanturine in difficulty.*	*Vessel escorted to harbour.*
22.12.43	*Eastbourne*	*Search requested by Royal Navy for possible survivors.*	*Area searched, only debris found.*
30.12.43*	Newhaven	American bomber crashed into sea.	Fishing boat Little Old Lady assisted with rescue of four crew.
30.12.43	*Hastings, Eastbourne & Pevensey (Shore boat).*	*American bomber crashed in Pevensey Bay.*	*Crew of aircraft rescued with assistance of other vessels.*

1944

23.01.44	Eastbourne	British aircraft reported to have come down into sea.	No crew found, but a single dingy was salvaged.
24.01.44	*Shoreham*	*Landing craft in difficulty*	*Assistance given.*
03.02.44	*Selsey*	*British aircraft seen to crash into the sea.*	*Injured pilot rescued.*
05.03.44*	*Rye*	*American fighter seen to crash into sea.*	*Fishing vessel FE152 rescued pilot and salvaged equipment.*
10.03.44	Hastings	Fishing vessel RX133 Lady Violet in difficulty	Boat and crew of 2 saved and seen to safety.
24.03.44*	*Hastings*	*Two boys stranded by the incoming tide.*	*Both rescued by rowing boat and fishing vessel RX 47.*
11.06.44	*Eastbourne*	*Aircraft reported crashed into sea.*	*One injured airman brought ashore from air-sea rescue plane.*
14.06.44	Hastings	Aeroplane crashed into sea.	Crew rescued by Royal Navy mine-sweepers and rescue launch.
17.06.44	Hastings	American aircraft reported in sea.	Pilot rescued by passing merchant vessel.
19.06.44	Hastings	British fighter aircraft crashed off St. Leonards.	Pilot rescued.
10.07.44	Shoreham	Landing craft in difficulty six miles south west of harbour.	Lifeboat attended and escorted landing craft and rescue tug.
24.07.44	Hastings	American Mustang fighter	No crew found, but equipment salvaged.

THEY ALSO SERVE

crashed into sea.

29.07.44	Hastings	American fighter crashed two and half miles off Hastings.	Wreckage seen, but no crew found.
28.08.44*	Selsey	British bomber crashed eight miles from coast.	Eight crew rescued by fishing boat.
03.11.44	*Newhaven*	*H.M. Drifter Supporter in difficulty.*	*Boat and crew of 12 assisted and saved.*
04.11.44	*Newhaven*	*S.S. Marcoz run aground at Rottingdean.*	*Lifeboat crew assisted in putting crew back on board for salvage.*
05.11.44	*Shoreham*	*Landing craft L.C.T. 532 signalling for help.*	*Landing craft and rescue tug escorted to Newhaven.*
17.11.44	*Hastings*	*Landing craft in difficulty off Pett Level.*	*Area searched, but landing craft had gone ashore at Galloways.*
17.11.44	*Selsey*	*Landing craft in difficulty.*	*Lifeboat launched, but landing craft had gone ashore.*
16.12.44	*Shoreham*	*S.S. Chorzow in difficulties*	*Crew put on board and escorted steamer to Shoreham.*
17.12.44	*Shoreham*	*S.S. Chorzow again in difficulty and beached.*	*Lifeboat stood by boat to rescue crew.*

<u>1945</u>

23.01.45	Selsey	S.S. Runnelstone of London in difficulty.	Lifeboat rendered assistance and stood by.
02.02.45	*Selsey*	*Naval floating crane in difficulty in Hayling Bay.*	*Crane and tug escorted to safety.*
21.03.45	*Shoreham*	*R.A.F. Salvage vessel Dutch Lady in difficulty.*	*Escorted to the safety of Littlehampton harbour.*
16.04.45	Shoreham	Private boat in trouble.	Boat saved.
21.04.45	Selsey	Canoe with two occupants on board missing at sea.	Area searched. Nothing found.
21.04.45	Shoreham	British Spitfire crashed into sea and blew up.	Wreckage found, no crew were seen.
26.04.45	*Shoreham*	*Boat adrift west of Worthing Pier failing to answer signals.*	*No persons on boat which was brought to shore.*
28.04.45	Hastings	Fishing punt with two crew had failed to return.	Lifeboat launched, but persons rescued by other fishing boat.

THEY ALSO SERVED

FURTHER READING

Bates, L.M.	**The Thames on Fire,**	*Terence Dalton Limited, 1985.*
Bickers, R.T.	**The Battle of Britain - The greatest battle in the history of air warfare,**	
		Salamander Books, 1990.
Brann, Christian.	**The Little Ships of Dunkirk.**	*Collectors Books Limited, 1989.*
Farr, Grahame.	**Grahame Farr Lifeboat Archives;**	
	Volume 15 - Kent & Rye	
	Volume 16 - East Sussex	
	Volume 17 - West Sussex	*RNLI Library Archives, Poole.*
Franks, Norman L.R.	**RAF Fighter Command Losses.**	*Midland Counties Publications Ltd, 1997.*
Humphrey, George.	**Wartime Eastbourne.**	*Beckett Features, 1989.*
Marsden, Peter.	**The Historic Shipwrecks of South-East England - A Diver's Guide.**	*Jarrold Colour Publications, 1987.*
McDonald, Kendall.	**Dive Sussex - A Diver's Guide.**	*Underwater World Publications Ltd, 1989.*
Middleton, Commander E.W.	**Great Sea Rescues, Vol. 2.**	*New English Library, 1976.*
Plummer, Russell.	**The Ships that saved an Army.**	*Patrick Stephens Limited, 1990.*
Ramsey, Winston G. (Ed).	**The Battle of Britain Then & Now.**	*Battle of Britain Prints, 1980.*
Ramsey, Winston G. (Ed).	**The Blitz Then & Now, Volume 1.**	*Battle of Britain Prints, 1989.*
Ramsey, Winston G. (Ed).	**The Blitz Then & Now, Volume 2.**	*Battle of Britain Prints, 1989.*
Ramsey, Winston G. (Ed).	**The Blitz Then & Now, Volume 3.**	*Battle of Britain Prints, 1990.*
Saunders A. & Burgess P.	**Battle over Sussex, 1940.**	*Middleton Press, 1990.*
Unknown.	**The Lifeboat Service at War, 1939-1945.**	*The Royal National Lifeboat Institution, 1945.*
Unknown.	**The Journal of the Royal National Lifeboat Institution Volume 31.**	
		The Royal National Lifeboat Institution.
Unknown.	**War Illustrated, volume 2**, page 411.	*April 19th 1940.*
Unknown.	**War Illustrated, volume 9**, page 590.	*January 18th, 1946.*

THEY ALSO SERVED